No Higher Calling

No Higher Calling

Joseph N. Hunt

Review and Herald Publishing Association
Washington, D.C.

This book was
Edited by Richard W. Coffen
Designed by Alan Forquer

Printed in U.S.A.

Library of Congress Cataloging in Publication Data

Hunt, Joseph N., 1928-
No higher calling.

1. Christian literature—Publication and distribution. 2. Evangelistic work. 3. Seventh-day Adventists. I. Title.
BR117.H79 253.7 81-11913
ISBN 0-8280-0064-6 AACR2

Table of Contents

Section One

No Higher Calling

Why Publishing?
Key Instruments for Harvest
Littera Scripta Manet
Primacy of Print
Of Special Importance

Why Publishing?

"Write the vision, and make it plain upon tables, that he may run that readeth it" (Hab. 2:2).

While the human mind still possessed the vigor of Eden oral communication sufficed. For centuries Adam or Enoch could pass on by word of mouth to each succeeding generation the knowledge of the Fall and of God's plan of redemption. But as man's vital force waned his mind became more degenerate, more prone to forget. Finally, God found it necessary to write His law on tables of stone. He also directed Moses to record His dealings with man from the beginning. And since that time anything that was important for man to remember He directed His servants to preserve for posterity.

For this very reason—to make sure that man would not forget—scribes in Israel copied the Scriptures with meticulous care. God likewise moved the Waldenses to copy the Scriptures by hand, and in the mid-1400s He gave Gutenberg the inventive genius to develop the first machine to print with movable type. By the middle of the 1800s God provided the high-speed presses with which to give His final warning clearly and quickly to all the world. Then, to make doubly sure mankind would understand, He sent His last-day prophet with specific instruction to "make known to others what I have revealed to you" (*Early Writings*, p. 20).

Publishing was, in fact, urged upon the infant Adventist Church before she had learned to walk. Ellen White told her husband in 1848: "'You must begin to print a little paper and send it out to the people. Let it be small at first; but as the people read, they will send you means with which to print, and it will be a success from the first. From this small beginning it was shown to me to be like streams of light that went clear round the world.'"—*Colporteur Ministry*, p. 1.

At that time the toddling church's resources could barely sustain its life. Her leaders would have to choose, as Ellen White did for her own child, between the "milk" and the "cloth." Even the ordinarily courageous Captain Bates did not feel they could or should start a regular printing venture. Some seven months passed by, and James White decided to mow a field of hay in order to earn the money for printing. But as he started to leave, Ellen White received another message. She saw that God did not want him then to go out and earn money "but that he must write, write, write" (*Life Sketches*, p. 126), and speed the message on its way.

It almost seemed that God had sent His most powerful angel to take James White by the shoulders, place him at his writing desk, and put the pen in his hand. The young church must put first things first. She must establish that which would produce the quickest growth and provide for her the most permanent strength and power. So our pioneers moved ahead with the first issue of *Present Truth*, published in July, 1849. Just three years later—eight years before we had a name—a printing house, the denomination's first institution, was established.

Ellen White explains it beautifully: "Our publishing work was established by the direction of God and under His special supervision. It was designed to accomplish a specific purpose. Seventh-day Adventists have been chosen by God as a peculiar people, separate from the world. By the great cleaver of truth He has cut them out from the quarry of the world and brought them into connection with Himself. He has made them His representatives and has called them to be ambassadors for Him in the last work of salvation. The greatest wealth of truth ever entrusted to mortals, the most solemn and fearful warnings ever sent by God to man, have been committed to them to be given to the world; and in the accomplishment of this work our publishing houses are among the most effective agencies."—*Testimonies*, vol. 7, p. 138.

God dared not allow a message of such solemn import to depend on the living preacher alone. It must go more quickly and endure more permanently than the spoken word.

In the same testimony Ellen White declares that our publications are to do the same work for the world that John the Baptist's message did for the Jewish nation—"prepare a people to meet God." These publishing institutions in every land are to accomplish the work of the angels flying in the midst of heaven. "From them is to go forth the terrible denunciation: 'Babylon is fallen, is fallen . . .' (Rev. 14:8). They are represented by the third angel that followed, 'saying with a loud voice, If any man worship the beast and his image, and receive his mark in his forehead, or in his hand, the same shall drink of the wine of the wrath of God' (verses 9, 10). And in a large degree through our publishing houses is to be accomplished the work of that other angel who comes down from heaven with great power and who lightens the earth with his glory."—*Ibid.*, p. 140.

The publishing of these messages not only is the chief instrument in giving the call "Come out of her, my people," but it is also a powerful means of preparing the members to stand undeviating against the final delusive onslaughts of the enemy. "Though the minister may faithfully present the message, the people are not able to retain it all. The printed page is therefore essential, not only in awakening them to the importance of the truth for this time, but in rooting and grounding them in the truth and establishing them against deceptive error. Papers and books are the Lord's means of keeping the message for this time continually before the people. In enlightening and confirming souls in the truth the publications will do a far greater work than can be accomplished by the ministry of the word alone."—*Colporteur Ministry*, p. 100.

We need both subscription and trade literature. Subscription books will awaken others to the knowledge of truth. Trade books will confirm them and establish them in the truth. Both the reading convert and the reading member are the strongest. Both the literature for the public and the literature for the church are "the Lord's means for keeping the message for this time continually before the people." Indeed the very strength of the church is determined by the quality products from her presses.

But why clothe our books in such beautiful and expensive garb? Why such fine-quality print, paper, and artwork? Shouldn't we emphasize quantity, the inexpensive newsprint, giveaway type of literature? Why sell a dressed-up LTD when a stripped-down Pinto might do the job? Both, of course, are essential. We must produce some publications economically so that we can scatter them by the millions like the leaves of autumn. But George King was right when he insisted that our first subscription book, *Thoughts on Daniel and the Revelation*, be illustrated beautifully and bound attractively. Customers would value and not discard a quality publication for which they had invested their hard-earned money. As a *Bible Readings* customer indignantly told her minister when he demanded that she burn that "Advent" book, "Not on your life! I paid good money for that book!" A giveaway edition might have been quickly consigned to the wastebasket or fireplace. But when families invest a sizable amount in our books or sets, they treasure them permanently on their bookshelves. And these books, accumulated in millions of homes, at the time of test "will be sought for and read" and will help convert more than one thousand in a single day.

What makes the printed page so effective? Why did it have priority at the beginning and why is it to have priority at the close of God's message? The reasons are clear. It most permanently witnesses for the truth. Although silent, it persists in saying the same thing over and over again. The reader may lay it aside in disgust, but when he picks it up again, the message has not changed. It gives the trumpet a certain sound and keeps on sounding it until the close of probation. And the one who finds the truth through books usually feels that he has discovered it himself, that it is his idea. Considering the independent spirit of man, it is a vital factor. It explains why "many minds can be reached in no other way" (*ibid.*, p. 148). Elder Theodore Carcich tersely explains: "No other agent penetrates so deeply, abides so persistently, witnesses so daringly, and influences so irresistibly as gospel literature."

The publishing work played a major role in the beginning of the Advent message, the vanguard of the truth on every continent and in every land. It is destined by sure prophetic decree to be God's special tool in the finishing of the message. As the front line advances, the entire army advances. When the publishing work moves forward, the church moves forward. Where the publishing work is strong, God's church is strong. The church dares not neglect that which provides her most effective power. She must keep on writing the vision and making it plain upon tables. "The church must give her attention to the canvassing work. . . . Then will she go forth 'fair as the moon, clear as the sun, and terrible as an army with banners.' "—*Ibid.*, p. 7.

Key Instruments for Harvest

The Seventh-day Adventist Church exists for a single reason—to preach the three angels' messages to every nation, kindred, tongue, and people. God has destined this prophetic movement for a specific task. Thus the publishing department exists solely to serve as a key agency for communicating this message. Ellen White makes it clear: "Our publishing work was established by the direction of God and under His special supervision. It was designed to accomplish a specific purpose. . . . The greatest wealth of truth ever entrusted to mortals, the most solemn and fearful warnings ever sent by God to man, have been committed to them [Seventh-day Adventists] to be given to the world; and in the accomplishment of this work our publishing houses are among the most effective agencies."—*Testimonies*, vol. 7, p. 138.

Publishing, then, was to become one of God's most effective instruments in proclaiming His last message to mankind. The printed word was to go forth to prepare a people to meet God, "the same work that was done by John the Baptist for the Jewish nation" (*ibid.*, p. 139). God intended that the publishing work would play a leading role in the giving of all three angels' messages, but particularly in giving the final, fourth angel's call of Revelation 18:1-4 (*ibid.*, p. 140).

God did not dare leave a message of such solemn import to the whims of man's finite judgment. Through His servant He personally gave special guidance and inspired the beautiful messages that would go out to the world. Through hundreds of pages of instruction He has guided writers, editors, printers, managers, and literature evangelists. From the editor's mind to the literature evangelist's hands to the homes of the people God intends to maintain a holy, effective channel.

Thus God instructed James and Ellen White to begin to publish. He promised that the printed pages would go like streams of light clear around the world. From that tiny stack of 1,000 copies of *Present Truth*, Seventh-day Adventist publishing has grown to veritable mountains of literature—more than $100,000,000 worth produced in a single year! Today, as a result of following God's prophetic blueprint, a mighty army of literature evangelists 16,000 strong march across our world divisions. They witness to at least 600,000 men, women, and children every day. In 1979, 19,633 persons joined the church as a result of literature evangelism. No other church has such a ministry. Through God's special direction and insistence it stands as a unique feature of Adventism's outreach to all nations.

So let's keep marching. The ring of every doorbell should remind us that we are God's key instruments for giving His last message and for bringing in the final harvest.

"The power of the press can hardly be overestimated. It has been truly called the right arm of our strength. Let the publishing houses be sustained, and the message of truth be sent out to all the nations of the earth."—*Review and Herald*, May 16, 1882.

Littera Scripta Manet

Littera scripta manet, the Latin words on the National Archives seal, seemed to leap out and strike fire in my soul. We had just watched our loved ones from the Midwest as they looked for the first time at the precious milestone documents of American history. All documents are carefully guarded and preserved under glass, the most valuable being lowered each evening into a huge bomb-proof vault. The Declaration of Independence, the Constitution, the Louisiana Purchase treaty, the Emancipation Proclamation, even former President Nixon's one-sentence letter of resignation—everything important to the nation is preserved there in permanent, written form. On the way out, when we glanced back to the poster at the entrance, we had a deeper appreciation of the Latin motto. The English translation stood out in stark simplicity next to quaint emblems of ink pot and quill: "THE WRITTEN WORD ENDURES."

As though echoing from one stately pillar of the Archives edifice to another, the words kept ringing in my heart. I could hear God's voice verifying this to His prophets of old: "Write the vision, and make it plain upon tables, that he may run that readeth it" (Hab. 2:2). I could hear Him assuring His modern-day messenger, " 'The messages for these last days shall be written in books, and shall stand immortalized.' "—*Selected Messages,* book 1, p. 32. And deep inside I thanked Him for calling us and for entrusting us with this most enduring and significant ministry, the ministry of the printed page.

"The written word endures!" As one aptly expressed it, "The preacher writes his words on water, but the writer carves his words in stone." Ellen White agreed: " 'A sermon may be preached and soon forgotten, but a book remains.' "—*Life Sketches*, p. 382. The books distributed ten, twenty, even fifty years ago are still preaching. The books you sell or give away today will keep turning souls to Christ until He comes. Could any work on earth be more lasting or more satisfying?

In the final sentence of his eulogy, Author Robert H. Davis eloquently asserts the endurance of the printed page: " 'And I shall never die until all things return to the immutable dust. I am the printing press.' "

J. D. Snider, whose vision gave us our beloved *Bible Story* set, put it this way: "Fixing thought in permanent form is the most wonderful of all man's accomplishments. His cities vanish, his governments fall, his most massive monuments crumble and decay, but his books, the children of his brain, live on."—*I Love Books*, pp. 30, 31.

Ministers of the printed page, let this grand realization electrify your whole being your first waking moment of every day! Let it quicken your pace as you hasten from home to home! Let it be your last gratifying thought before you slip into the deserving slumber of the night! You are handling the immortal, that which God considers the most persistent, the most permanent, and the most powerful witness for the finishing of His work. Thank God that He has made you a literature worker, one of Heaven's special messengers. May these words be emblazoned forever across the tender scroll of your heart: *Littera scripta manet*—the written word endures!

Primacy of Print

Several speakers, including Sister White, had addressed large and attentive audiences at the Rome, New York, camp meeting on September 12, 1875. The very next night Ellen White dreamed that a heavenly messenger appeared in her room immediately after she had finished speaking. He warned that without the printed page " 'your efforts will prove nearly fruitless.' " The angel spoke of the power of the press to move the minds and hearts of the people. He urged that the entire church become involved in circulating literature "in all the cities and villages of the land. Here is missionary work for all." Some should be trained to give their full time to the work. The very words of this heavenly messenger are recorded in *Life Sketches*, page 217: " 'Many minds can be reached in no other way. *Here is true missionary work in which labor and means can be invested with the best results*." (Italics supplied.)

Look at that last sentence again. Did you know that God had given such definite, clear counsel regarding the value of literature and books? All Seventh-day Adventists like to get the most for their money. This inspired statement clearly affirms how both labor and means can bring the best and most lasting results. There need be no doubt. Let us assure our fellow believers that in this work—purchasing and distributing our literature—time, labor, and means can be invested with the *best results*.

But some may ask, "Can't we get just as large returns by investing in buildings, public evangelism, or other phases of the work?" Jacques Zurcher, missionary to Basutoland and head printer for the Paris Missionary Society, can answer that question and tell us why the church should give priority to literature. His words were quoted recently in the *World Christian Digest:*

"Why is the printed page so powerful, one may ask? First of all, the printed page can go where no missionary can travel. It requires no maintenance. It never falls sick. It requires no furlough with its often high traveling expenses. It does not need a pension scheme. It does not weigh heavily on a missionary society's budget. It is the missionary par excellence, to use a French expression. The page can be left alone to do its work, once it has been handed to a person to read. Further, the printed page can be secured and read in secret. It gets full attention in quiet hours. It knows no language barriers, no race restriction. . . . The printed page is one of the most economical means of carrying out our Lord's commission. Gospel literature can be produced cheaply. It can travel at little expense over long distances."

As balanced literature workers we must continue to encourage investments in churches, schools, and every phase of God's evangelistic program. But let us never forget, or allow our fellow church members to forget, the power of the press. "'Many minds can be reached in no other way.'"—*Life Sketches*, p. 217. The printed page is the most economical, permanent way to give God's message. Investing time and money in literature brings the greatest returns for eternity.

Of Special Importance

When I was only 16, the Lord made me feel the power and the importance of our large message books. As my partner and I planned for our second summer of canvassing, our consciences would not permit us to sell mostly health literature. We determined to follow the Lord's counsel, so we memorized a new canvass for a full-message book.

We must have presented quite a spectacle when we first started out. The publishing department secretary had arranged for special bikes with oversized baskets fitted above the undersized front wheels. It was tough going over those many miles of dusty Iowa roads. We had to depend entirely on God and the farmers' hospitality for food and lodging. I have never felt more lonely, more tired, or more hungry. Yet I was never happier, because I knew I was helping to deliver God's message.

Later, as a publishing secretary, I noticed that the best soul winners were the literature evangelists who sold *The Great Controversy*. Children's sets had become popular and were easier to sell, but that inner voice kept reminding me, "Children's books should be entering wedges, just as God planned the medical books to be."

During my next Big Week I promised God that I would include a *Great Controversy* or *Desire of Ages* with every set. When I asked my first prospect, a fine German Lutheran farmer, which of these masterpieces he would prefer with his set, he immediately responded, "How much would it be for both?" As I completed writing the receipt for the children's Bible books plus these two inspired books I breathed a few words of thanks to God for clearly revealing His divine pleasure. I also silently pledged that these books would ever form part of my unit of sale.

In Africa I saw the power that attends Ellen White's books when they are translated into other languages. Thousands of souls in East Africa accepted the message through the sale of *Vita Kuu*. In Swahili *vita* means battle and *kuu* means chief. So *The Great Controversy* in East Africa is known as "The Chief Battle Between Christ and Satan."

Would you like to know why the Africa Herald Publishing House continues printing a picture of a sword on *The Great Controversy* cover? Shortly after *Vita Kuu* was published, Tanzania colporteur James Gunza met a Catholic teacher who presented this urgent plea: "For three years I have searched everywhere for a book that I saw in a dream. It had a picture of a sword on the cover. If you can get me that book, I will pay you any price."

When James Gunza brought out *Vita Kuu*, the Catholic teacher reached for it like a starving man reaching for bread. "This is the book! This is the book!" he cried.

He read night and day, and in a short while he decided to burn all his beads, crucifixes, and images, as the man in the dream said he should, and he began to keep the Sabbath. God had prepared this man for the message of *Vita Kuu* and had given him the dream even before our brethren at the publishing house had decided to print the picture of the sword on the cover.

God revealed to Ellen White that "the angels of God would prepare the way for these books in the hearts of the people" (*Colporteur Ministry*, p. 124). "These books must be regarded as of special importance."—*Ibid.*, p. 123. "These books contain truth for this time—truth that is to be proclaimed in all parts of the world. Nothing is to hinder their sale."—*Ibid.*, p. 124.

Won't you make sure you are following the blueprint and that your briefcase always carries these precious books?

Section Two

A Deeper Commitment

Swords Unsheathed
Satan's Subtle Strategy
Glimpses of Gold
Our Sacred Honor
Qualities of a King
Their Commitment
Priority for Power
The Orient's Undaunted

Swords Unsheathed

The swords of George Washington form a striking display in the museum at his Mount Vernon, Virginia, home. Neatly typed words beneath the swords give the names of his nephews. Upon Washington's death each nephew received one of these prized weapons. Washington's will regarding this special legacy reveals the fortitude and character of the United States' first president: "These swords are accompanied with an injunction not to unsheathe them for the purpose of shedding blood except it be for self-defense or in defense of their country and its rights; and in the latter case, to keep them unsheathed, and prefer falling with them in their hands, to the relinquishment thereof." Don't you think these words could aptly describe the duty of the true Christian soldier? His sword will *never* be sheathed or relinquished until the day of complete and final victory.

The apostle Paul stands unrivaled as an example of this unremitting vigilance: "Endure hardness," he urges, "as a good soldier of Jesus Christ" (2 Tim. 2:3). Paul was never wishy-washy or halfhearted. He stood strong and brave, with the whole armor of God, and shortly before the executioner's sword descended he bravely declared, "I have fought a good fight, I have finished my course, I have kept the faith" (chap. 4:7). He held the sword of truth aloft to the last moment of his life.

Persecution nearly exterminated the Waldenses, but in

1689 Henri Arnaud led a band of eight hundred soldiers back into their beloved valleys. However, the brave little army had to fight for possession of the land. The vicious battles that ensued caused the morale of some Waldensian valiants to wane despite the Vaudois' successes. So on Sunday, September 11, in a mountain meadow just outside the town of Bobi, Henri Arnaud challenged the surviving soldiers with a pledge of loyalty. After hearing Arnaud read the oath, the soldiers raised their hands to heaven and swore that they would uphold and maintain their faith to the last drop of their blood. Filled with renewed spirit and despite overwhelming odds, these valiant hundreds put thousands to flight. They would never yield their faith. They would never sheathe their swords.

From the time of her teen-age conversion to the moment of her death, Ellen White never faltered in her warfare for Christ. When she was 85, she visited Pacific Union College and spoke to the students. "I was young like you when God called me to His work. I put my armor on, and I have never taken it off. Young people, put your hand to the plow and never turn back." Then she paused a moment and gave her final testimony: "My work is almost done, my strength is not what it was once, but so long as I live I shall never take my armor off."—*Facts and Comments About the Spirit of Prophecy*, p. 6.

Our great Commander has called us to arms in the final battle against Satan and sin. He has placed the weapons in our hands. There can be no compromise, no release. It is never safe to dabble in détente with the devil. As did the pioneer heroes of the past, so we must allow His Spirit to keep us faithful. We must never lay aside the true bookman's armor. We must never sheathe His sword of truth.

Satan's Subtle Strategy

"All my life I have wanted to be a colporteur," a good Adventist brother assured the publishing director, "but I want to get to the place where I don't have to depend on it for my living. I want to do it just to give the message and not for the money." Year after year he pleaded the same excuse to the publishing leader's appeal. Finally, when he didn't have to trust the Lord for his living, he presented himself with a filled-in application. "Now I can do it. I am retiring with a good Social Security pension." But the required physical examination revealed unsuspected symptoms of cancer. Before the fourth Social Security check arrived, our good brother was laid to rest. Satan had cleverly rationalized another soul out of years of happy service.

Ellen White warns of the evil one's most successful strategy: "Presumption is a common temptation, and as Satan assails men with this, he obtains the victory nine times out of ten."—*Testimonies*, vol. 4, p. 44.

It is difficult to distinguish the counterfeit from the true. Therefore, this temptation is almost 100 percent effective. "Presumption is Satan's counterfeit of faith."—*The Desire of Ages*, p. 126.

In presumption Satan uses God's promises and suggests noble motives to excuse us from or to postpone our duty to God and to His work. Thus he sought to urge Christ in His humanity "over the line of trust to presumption" (*Selected Messages*, book 1, p. 282). He offered our Saviour an easier way to witness and to win the world back to its allegiance to God. "Cast thyself down," Satan urged (Matt. 4:6). "All these things will I give thee" (verse 9).

The wily tempter hasn't changed. Today he cleverly

allures us into thinking it would be easier and just as important to take up another line of work. We allow him to twist us into believing that our own selfish plans are God's plans. He stands by us as he did our Saviour to misquote the Scriptures and the *Testimonies*, suggesting nice and noble motives for choosing an easier way to do God's will.

I remember how he worked to turn back one of my veteran literature workers who was passing through a financial crisis. Satan spoke through a respected counselor, who encouraged him to take a salaried sales job. "Brother," he advised, "you have to think of your family." No doubt the picture of "all these things" included more time at home with his family, more time to give Bible studies, and so on.

Now for nearly twenty-five years my friend has sold specialty items—key chains, calendars, and other advertising trinkets. He has done well financially, but he has missed a lifetime of service and the joy of delivering God's printed message to at least twenty-five thousand families. Also his own children could never know the privilege that only a colporteur's child can know, that of growing up praying and sacrificing that "my daddy" might help many people get ready for Jesus' coming.

But because the Man Christ Jesus prevailed, literature evangelists today don't have to succumb to Satan's most subtle strategy. The same faith that brought Jesus victory will give us victory. *The Desire of Ages*, page 126, assures us that "only he who has true faith is secure against presumption." As long as we maintain a firm, close relationship with Jesus, Satan can never compel us to yield to presumptuous sin or to give up God's work. No matter how cleverly or attractively he pictures "all these things," let's make sure he doesn't beguile us out of the crown and inheritance God has reserved for every faithful literature worker.

Glimpses of Gold

It was a mind-boggling sight—real bricks of solid gold—pure, shining gold! Pastor A. M. du Plessis, South African Union publishing director, had kindly scheduled this exciting visit to the Welkom gold mines of Orange Free State. Deep underground we watched as miners and modern machines dug out the precious ore. Hundreds of tons of ore and the labor of 10,000 workers are required each day to produce less than two bricks of gold. With a little encouragement the manager ordered the week's store of gold to be brought out of the strongroom and placed on the display table. From these nine bricks we built a little pyramid of gold, a dazzling array worth more than three million dollars. As our cameras clicked, enabling us to take it all with us on film, I thought again of God's assurance, "I will make a man more precious than fine gold; even a man than the golden wedge of Ophir" (Isa. 13:12).

During the scheduled safari through the continent that probably housed the land of Ophir, I kept thinking: Africa's most precious treasure is not really gold or diamonds, but rather the reflections of Christ's unselfish love in the lives of her men and women.

At the Zambesi Union publishing institute I met a tall, noble African with graying hair. He lives in Botswana and walks many miles while carrying heavy boxes of books on his head. The joy of delivering Jesus' message constrains him to endure any burden or hardship.

In Tanzania I listened to an army of literature evangelists sing their own beautifully composed theme song, "A Thousand in One Day Through the 'Ujumbe wa Kimya' [silent messenger]."

In Kenya I watched Paul Jensen lead a chorus of three

hundred literature evangelists as they chanted in unison a canvass in Swahili for *The Great Controversy*. What a glorious sound! Here, indeed, is Africa's most precious treasure.

In Zaire I witnessed a miracle of surrender. Responding to God's appeal to stay faithful, an educated young man insisted that I take a thick manila envelope that contained all his certificates and diplomas. With tears streaming down his cheeks he testified that these had become his idol and that he had been tempted to get an even higher degree and go into another profession. But as he contemplated his Saviour on the cross he decided instead to surrender his selfish plans. He would stay by God's special work.

One of the most valuable lives of all ended at an obscure village in northern Zambia on May 1, 1873. There David Livingstone died on his knees, praying for Africa. We found the spot after a torturous all-day pilgrimage in Dale Thomas' Peugeot. Together we bowed beside the humble monument and with tears prayed that we might serve unselfishly, as did Livingstone. David Livingstone traveled 29,000 miles through primitive African bush and declared, "I never made a sacrifice; I only paid back a small part of the great debt owing to our God for the gift of His dear Son." If only he could see today the "gold" all along the trails he blazed in Africa—the thousands of African messengers marching in his footsteps and reaching out to the remaining dark corners!

Surely these glimpses of African gold can inspire us to allow more of the pure gold of Jesus' love to shine out through us.

Our Sacred Honor

More than two centuries ago the delegates to the Continental Congress debated a special document. It spoke eloquently of the inalienable rights of all men to "life, liberty, and the pursuit of happiness." Late in the afternoon of July 4 church bells began to ring, signaling the adoption of the Declaration of Independence. Ultimately, fifty-six courageous leaders signed this declaration: "With a firm reliance on the protection of divine Providence, we mutually pledge to each other our Lives, our Fortunes, and our sacred Honor."

Notice that these men pledged more than their lives and possessions. They pledged their sacred honor. They had given their word, and they could not turn back. These patriots totally committed themselves to the cause of freedom. Such commitment reminds me of the spirit our own denominational pioneers showed at the launching of a greater cause, that of declaring eternal freedom to all mankind. Like the signers of the Declaration of Independence, our pioneers willingly laid everything on the altar.

In our mind's eye we picture James White as a strong warrior in the field. We remember his rugged hands—calloused from swinging the scythe, or bleeding from carrying rock to build a railroad siding. We see him limping those eight miles again and again from Rocky Hill to Middletown, Connecticut, to publish the first issues of *Present Truth*. Yet in the early 1850s as he struggled with poverty, excessive labor, and the envy of brethren, he cried out to his wife, " 'I cannot go any farther. I have written a note for the paper, stating that I shall publish no more.' "—*Life Sketches*, p. 140. But before James White could deliver that note, God instructed him through Ellen White that Satan was trying to drive him from the work. "I was shown," she declared, "that we must continue to publish, and the Lord would sustain us."—*Ibid.*, p. 141. The sacred honor of God was at stake. His printed word must go out to the world!

Think of the toughness in the character of pioneer evangelist John Loughborough. For many months he worked four days a week on farms for only one dollar a day. Then on weekends he conducted evangelistic meetings in tents and schoolhouses. When he was finally paid for his preaching it amounted to only four dollars a week. Financial necessity and discouragement led him to join the Waukon, Iowa, Adventists and return to the carpenter's trade. When the Whites visited Waukon and called for repentance and a return to the work, John Loughborough rose and testified, " 'I have laid up my hammer! I have driven the last nail! Henceforth my hand shall hold the sword of the Spirit, and never give it up. So help me, God!' " He had pledged his sacred honor. He would keep his word.

Later, in 1885 at the European Council, the newly recruited colporteurs told why our literature could not be sold in Catholic Europe on the same plan as in America. They urged that they be granted salaries. But Ellen White repeatedly declared that God had shown her that books could be successfully sold in Europe. " 'Remember, brethren,' " she assured them, " 'in every perplexity, that God has angels still. . . . When the work goes hard, and you become discouraged and are tempted to abandon it, take your Bible, bow upon your knees before God, and say, "Here, Lord, Thy word is pledged." Throw your weight upon His promises, and every one of them will be fulfilled.' "—*Ibid.*, p. 285.

Just as certainly God has pledged His word for your success today. The honor of His throne is at stake. Will you likewise lay your sacred honor on the line and pledge to stay by until His cause triumphs in the earth?

Qualities of a King

During 1980 literature evangelists everywhere thought a lot about the life of George King, because that year was the one-hundred-year jubilee honoring the first Adventist literature evangelist. Our lives are enriched as we take a closer look at that man. What was George King really like? Why was he so successful? Was it his education or IQ? No, the records show that he had only eight or nine years of education. Was it his speaking ability? "Uncle Richard" Godsmark proved that he had no special talent in this respect. Was it the way he dressed? Certainly clothes did not make this man. Mrs. Godsmark spent several days getting his clothing in respectable condition before he started. Was it his size, his commanding appearance? Hardly. He weighed only 133 pounds, was 5 feet 8 inches tall, and was deaf in one ear.

But George King had character. He was visible proof that "what a man is has more influence than what he says," and that "it is our own character and experience that determine our influence upon others" (*The Ministry of Healing*, p. 469). The influence and work of his life also verified that "the world does not so much need men of great intellect as of noble character" (*Education*, p. 225).

The following appeals for colporteurs penned by George King for the columns of the *Review and Herald* reveal the character of the man. Read these excerpts from his articles, and notice how they imply the King Jesuslike qualities in his life.

"A call is made for canvassers—for men who will speak boldly and act wisely in the closing scenes of earth's history; for men who will volunteer their services till the work is done; for men who will hold on, in the fear of God, when the work goes hard—not for people who compose the 'floating element' of society, who will work till they have begun to learn how, and then give up, but for men who will keep up a course of study as they work, and thus brighten up for whatever may be future duty; for men who will make a grand success of life."—Jan. 24, 1882. "Having followed the business for years, and having met many of the best canvassers, I know that many of the difficulties exist only in name. . . . With patience and hard work, all the difficulties connected with the business can be overcome."—*Ibid.*

"While the *Signs* as a paper will soon be laid aside, the book [*Thoughts on Daniel and the Revelation*] will speak in its bound form . . . till the end of time. When, therefore, it is asked how this canvassing work is to be run, we say, with good reasons, . . . if there is a weak-kneed brother, let him break in on the *Signs;* but let all our able-bodied young and middle-aged men go to work nobly on *Thoughts on Daniel and the Revelation,* and 'grow like the cedar in Lebanon' for usefulness in the one great cause."—*Ibid.,* Aug. 21, 1883.

Yes, George King was *bold, courageous, persevering, and unflinching in the face of difficulties.*

This striking appeal appeared in the *Review* of August 22, 1882: "Lord Nelson, when about to open one of his important battles on the sea, had flying . . . [from his flagship so that all could see, the signal] 'England expects every man to do his duty.' In that battle victory perched upon the banners of those who acted upon that motto. . . . A little company will be found under the banner of 'the law of God and the testimony of Jesus,' part of whom will do their duty, and the rest, we fear, will be ready for duty just when it is too late, like Meroz, 'who came not up to the help of the Lord, to the help of the Lord, against the mighty.' All men are ready to do their duty sometime; but the successful man is ready at the right time. 'Curse ye Meroz.' "

George King was a diligent worker. He put duty first.

What a noble example for all of us who follow in his footsteps! Let us allow Christ to develop these qualities in our lives. We must let the character of the King shine through. Remember, "A noble, all-round character is not inherited. It does not come to us by accident. A noble character is earned by individual effort through the merits and grace of Christ."—*Christ's Object Lessons*, p. 331.

Won't you let these King Jesus qualities ennoble your life and make you men and women of influence and power?

Their Commitment

I am writing these lines at the site of the ancient College of the Waldenses. I'm sitting at one of the old stone tables around which the first missionary colporteurs were trained and on which they copied the Scriptures by hand. The Swiss and Greek literature workers have just finished kneeling around this meaningful "altar." They have renewed their commitment, and they have heartily sung together "A Mighty Fortress Is Our God."

While they descend the rocky trail to the village of Pra del Torno, something compels me to linger, to meditate a little longer about the lives and the shed blood of the true bookman's spiritual ancestors. Wylie called this spot the "inner sanctuary of the Waldensian temple." From here the first literature evangelist heroes went out to face the wrath of Rome. Could anyone find a higher inspiration point from which to send a challenge to God's modern bookman army?

As each group of Europe's book evangelists studies the history of the Waldenses, visits these monuments and caves, sees the rugged bulwarks of their defense and the steeps from which they were hurled, new resolves well up in each worker. "I'll never again murmur or complain." "I'll never again be content to attempt so little for the Master."

Three factors stand out boldly in the lives of these first missionary literature evangelists. These traits should challenge us all "to imitate their example of sacrifice and self-denial" (*Colporteur Ministry*, p. 99).

First, they lived by the Word of God. They disciplined themselves to learn the Bible. Most of the Waldensian missionary colporteurs could reproduce from memory the Psalms plus the entire New Testament. They lived so religiously by His "every word" that the priests accused them of making "a pope of the Bible." After Soldier-Pastor Henri Arnaud and his brave eight hundred reached the crest of the mountains above their valleys in 1689, they fell to their knees, lifted their arms to heaven, and solemnly pledged that the light of the Bible should never again be extinguished from their homelands. They had placed God's Word above all in their lives.

Second, they willingly suffered, sacrificed, and faced hardships for the cause of Christ. In the Waldensian Museum in Torre Pellice I read the dates of thirty-one different inquisitions against these faithful people. "And yet," Ellen White exclaims, even in their cold, hunger, and nakedness, "the scattered and homeless ones would assemble to unite their voices in singing, and praising God that they were accounted worthy to suffer for Christ's name. They encouraged and cheered one another, and were grateful for even their miserable retreat."—*Testimonies*, vol. 1, p. 371.

Third, these first missionary literature evangelists made a lifetime commitment to God's call. They never thought of going partway or of turning back. Cards and plaques placed on the wall just above this old stone table illustrate the completeness of their commitment. The words on one card explain, "They went out into the world by twos for their bitter and often perilous itinerant mission. Their mission lasted a lifetime until their force was spent, or until they fell to martyrdom." Two other plaques contain an unusual honor roll—a list of forty-nine names of those who met a martyr's fate, those who went out from this college but didn't come back.

May God give us more of their spirit of courage, stamina, love, and sacrifice!

Priority for Power

Commenting on Joshua's mighty prayer to stop the sun at Gibeon, Ellen White declares, "He did all that human energy could do, and then he cried in faith for divine aid. The secret of success is the union of divine power with human effort. Those who achieve the greatest results are those who rely most implicitly on the Almighty Arm. . . . The men of prayer are the men of power."—*Patriarchs and Prophets*, p. 509. Every great worker for God in every age habitually scheduled priority time for communion with God—for the study of His Word and for prayer.

One of the world's greatest preachers, Charles Spurgeon, put it this way, "Let your fleece lie on the threshing floor of supplication till it is wet with the dew of heaven."—Harold L. Calkins, *Master Preachers*, p. 49. In his autobiography he speaks eloquently of the minister's essential for power. "While the unformed minister is revolving upon the wheels of preparation, prayer is the tool of the great Potter by which He molds the vessel. All our libraries and studies are mere emptiness compared with our closets. We grow, we wax mighty, we prevail in private prayer."—*Ibid.*

Charles Finney, another powerful preacher and revivalist, habitually read his Bible on his knees. He suggested that even though we have the intellectual endowment of an angel, we should do nothing without these seasons of secret study and prayer. He testified of his complete dependence on God and a holy perseverance in prayer: " 'If even for a day or an hour I lost the spirit of grace and supplication, I found myself unable to preach with power and efficiency, or to win souls by personal conversation. . . . I would pray to God that He had made a promise to answer prayer and I could not and would not be denied.' "—Basil Miller, *Charles G. Finney*, p. 50.

Dwight L. Moody, famous evangelist who lessened Satan's harvest of lost souls by at least a million, lived a life of Bible study and prayer. His biographer, R. A. Torrey, tells of Moody's devotional life. "Out of a very intimate acquaintance with him, I wish to testify that he was a far greater pray-er than he was a preacher. Time and time again, he was confronted by obstacles that seemed insurmountable, but he always knew the way to surmount and overcome all difficulties. He knew the way to bring to pass anything that needed to be brought to pass. He knew and believed in the deepest depths of his soul that nothing was too hard for the Lord and that prayer could do anything that God could do."—Calkins, *op. cit.*, pp. 98, 99.

This is Christ's appointed way to power and success. Communion with God alone in the desert or on the mountain preceded every major triumph of Jesus' earthly life. Like all these great workers for God, we too must put first things first and experience anew this priority for power.

The Orient's Undaunted

I seemed compelled to come back again today to the graveside of Abram La Rue in Hong Kong's Happy Valley Cemetery. Yesterday more than 200 literature evangelists and leaders from all lands of the Orient gathered here. Lifting their hands to God, they committed their lives, as Abram La Rue so nobly committed his, to finishing God's work through the literature ministry. All is quiet now around his grave. On all sides I notice the graves of young seamen from many vessels, no doubt the very ships Abram La Rue visited and supplied with literature. He now rests peacefully among his customers, the sailors he so faithfully witnessed to for fifteen years in Hong Kong's harbor.

How did Abram La Rue work? What motivated him? How can we who follow in his footsteps recapture a little of his spirit and his fire? Abram La Rue faced opposition and conquered obstacles through the Word and the power of God. In several of his letters to the brethren he wrote of Hong Kong as being not only the best place on earth but also probably the most difficult place to sell religious books and to do missionary work.

It was especially difficult because other established missionaries bitterly opposed him and tried to turn the ships' officers against him and his publications. "They would tear them up and destroy them nightly, so I would take them out nights and put them in the next morning. . . . I was determined to keep them before the people. . . . I am sending them all over the China coast and Japan and also Siam. . . . The Lord has said, 'If He is for us, none can be against.' This I believe with all my heart, and He has also said, 'When the enemy shall come in like a flood, the Spirit of the Lord shall lift up a standard against him.' This I believe also, and I also believe they cannot do anything against the truth but for the truth."—Letter, Nov. 26, 1888.

The blessed hope of Christ's imminent return and Abram La Rue's burden to see all nations ready motivated his life. He longed to share his convictions with other missionaries in all the cities and countries of the Orient. In 1891 he discovered eighteen missionaries from London on the steamer *Rosetta*. They were headed for the interior of China. He took passage on the same ship as far as Shanghai in order to witness to them and to circulate literature in China.

Abram La Rue worked earnestly, untiringly, sacrificially. After his first year's work, he wrote to Elder White on May 9, 1899, that he had already visited more than four hundred ships. Again and again he pleaded for the brethren to send missionaries.

It would have been wonderful if this stalwart warrior could have seen the more than two hundred Abram La Rue Club members who met here in Hong Kong! If only he could know that they represent the nearly 4,000 literature evangelists who march across the countries of the Orient. He would have thrilled to meet one who had won more than one hundred souls and another who had seen more than fifty join the church, to have known that one hundred and sixty students were working in Hong Kong.

Someday soon the Life-giver's trumpet will sound, and Abram La Rue will step forth from his grave to meet his Lord. Through all eternity the Orient's undaunted witness will behold the results of his years of sacrificial service. May God give us, each one, more of his spirit and fire.

Section Three

Perseverance in Face of Difficulties

Eyes on the Ultimate
Playing Hurt
Heaven's MVPs
Invincible Determination
"I Fight to Win"
Above Infirmities
Five or Six Times

Eyes on the Ultimate

Elisha's servant at Dothan felt ready to despair. He could see only the Syrian horses and chariots that completely surrounded the city. Elisha, however, could see more and declared with confidence, "Fear not: for they that be with us are more than they that be with them" (2 Kings 6:16). Then Elisha asked the Lord to open the young man's eyes so that he, too, might see God's chariots of fire all around them.

How often we are like Elisha's servant! We allow obstacles to loom big on the horizon of our finite vision. Satan keeps our eyes on the immediate. He delights to see our minds overwhelmed with anxiety. But when the Holy Spirit fully takes charge, He opens our eyes. By His grace we can see, beyond the obstacles, the fiery chariots of Heaven's hosts protecting us and overruling all for ultimate triumph.

Our great need today is to possess the vision and the spirit of Elisha. He had a sense of God's ultimate purpose but no sense whatsoever of the obstacles in the way. And the same spirit has possessed the great achievers of all time. Alexander the Great saw only India's fabulous wealth and splendor. He didn't see the torturous march through the Khyber Pass, across rivers, over mountains, and through warlike nations. Napoleon saw Italy but not the Alps. Washington saw the Hessians at Trenton. A lesser-visioned man would have seen the ice-filled Delaware.

Literature workers face the horses and chariots of the

enemy every day. It would be easy for us to fix our eyes on problems and difficulties. But when our lives are in tune with Heaven and we see the fiery hosts of God's power and the ultimate 1,000-in-one-day harvest, no obstacle can ever force us to retreat.

For example, the gasoline shortage in various parts of the earth could pose an obstacle to ordinary workers, but it hasn't stopped literature evangelists. Warren Hewes tells how the literature evangelists in the Southern California Conference turned this obstacle into a blessing. While waiting in the long lines at gas stations they distributed advertising brochures from car to car! A. J. Oberholster writes how his workers face this problem in the Transvaal Conference, South Africa: "Petrol here costs almost 40 cents per liter, which is US$1.92 per gallon. This is very hard on our literature workers, but they are full of courage. One told me recently that even if he has to buy a bicycle he is not going to let the petrol situation take him out of the work God has called him to do."

With such noble men and women adversity never hinders. Poet Robert L. Byrd pictures how it works: "I saw today a struggling soul tossed wildly by a raging storm, But, facing toward a cherished goal, He braved the gale with courage warm. Those winds that sought to lay him low Served but to help him higher go."

As literature evangelists we must rise undaunted above all that now obstructs our way. We must think like Elisha. The royal chariots of fire roll along ahead of us, behind us, and beside us. We must keep our eyes off the immediate obstacles and on the glorious ultimate objectives.

Playing Hurt

Tony Green, return specialist of the Washington Redskins football team, had suffered a severe leg injury. But Tony stayed in the game and ran the 80- and 90-yard winning touchdowns. The sportscasters called it "playing hurt"—a heroic performance for the team in spite of pain.

Do you remember Fujimoto, of the Japanese Olympic gymnastic team? Shortly before the Olympics he had broken his knee. While he still remained confined to a hospital bed, his teammates surrounded him and insisted they could not win without him. Bob Richards described how Fujimoto, with a cast on his leg, achieved the greatest performance of his life. "Tears streaming down his face, his body wracked with pain, he went shooting off into a double-twisting, double-backed somersault, landing on his feet without the suggestion of a hurt; 9.5 went up on the board!" Fujimoto's performance in pain won the gold medal for his team.

The fighting spirit of these athletes reminds us of the divine Player and how He "played hurt" for the souls of men. How much did He hurt? How long and how well has He performed in the presence of pain? It started with the entrance of sin. "Through long ages God has borne the anguish of beholding the work of evil."—*Christ's Object Lessons*, p. 72.

Especially during His earthly life the hurts and insults were vicious and unremitting. "From the time when He was a babe in Bethlehem, He was continually assailed by the evil one. . . . Christ was made the mark of every weapon of hell."—*The Desire of Ages*, p. 116. All heaven hurt when human apathy offered only a crude stable for the royal birthplace. Herod's hatred forced the young king of heaven to start life as a refugee in a foreign land. During His childhood in Nazareth the taunts of His brothers and young companions constantly hurt Him. Later He felt the sting of the hateful opposition of the Pharisees and spies who dogged His footsteps.

In Gethsemane when He longed for human encouragement, it hurt to find His dearest friends asleep. The bloody sweat, the Father's presence withdrawn, and the broken heart hurt more deeply than we can ever understand. Can you imagine His look of hurt and disappointment at Judas' kiss of pretended sympathy and Peter's wretched denial? And, oh, how it hurt when the beings whom He had formed in His own image mocked Him, spat upon Him, scourged Him, and cried "Crucify Him!" A dismayed heavenly host awaited their Commander's call for help, but the piercing nails evoked only words of love and compassion.

Satan "could not discourage Him, or drive Him from a work He had come on earth to do. From the desert to Calvary, the storm of Satan's wrath beat upon Him, but the more mercilessly it fell, the more firmly did the Son of God cling to the hand of His Father, and press on in the bloodstained path."—*Ibid.*, p. 759. Jesus refused to stop "playing hurt." He would not turn back from vindicating His Father's character of love.

Fellow door-to-door workers, we too must face hurts, resistance, and disappointments. Satan has directed his hellish weapons against us. Will we allow the rebuffs and bruises to turn us aside? Or will we, like the Master, go on playing hurt without flinching, without letting the hurt show?

Heaven's MVPs

Few events trigger more excitement than a decisive home run in the World Series. Thousands of fans jump to their feet, wildly cheering, whistling, and shouting their approval. In 1973 the New York Yankees' home-run king, Reggie Jackson, was voted the MVP—the most valuable player of the World Series.

All of this fuss about a baseball champion got me to thinking about the much more exciting "game" that you and I are playing for heaven. What makes us valuable in the eyes of our Captain? Certain criteria—such as the number we are bringing "home"—remain the same, but often He who looks on the heart judges differently from man. Here are a few qualities that God values most. They make literature evangelists MVPs for heaven.

Pure, unselfish motivation would, no doubt, rank highest on the divine scale. It surrounds a literature evangelist like an aura of glory, affecting every transaction and every part of his daily program. Just as in our Master's earthly life, so our entire interest must center in others. Love must compel us to begin each day's work early and to hurry to reach as many souls as possible. Obsessed with the cause of hastening Jesus' return, we must never put our own comforts or interests first.

Revealing a Christlike kindness and humility would be another important criterion for heaven's MVPs. Unlike the worldly victor's acclamations of pride, God's successful bookperson ascribes all glory to the Lord. No matter how abusive or unkind others may be to us, we will "maintain a sweet, free, pleasant dignity" (*Colporteur Ministry*, p. 41). We will never retaliate under provocation. When God overrules and brings success, we recognize that heavenly beings have beaten back Satan's opposition. We know, as John the Baptist knew, that we are only a voice. We will not take any honor to ourselves. By being kind to the unappreciative and by humbly doing good without taking any credit, we bear in our characters the "insights of the royalty of heaven" (*Thoughts From the Mount of Blessing*, p. 75).

Working on in faith, oblivious to obstacles and disappointments, could well be the third quality most appreciated by Heaven. Elder W. H. Branson, former General Conference president, pictured the literature evangelist's role in this interesting way: "The evangelist has the backing of a team, a choir, or a quartet. He marches with the banners flying and the band playing, but the colporteur marches alone, without the band."

Like a lone commando or paratrooper we perform dangerous missions in the midst of enemy territory. We face the toughest opposition in one-to-one combat. Then we let other troops claim the victory and win the "captives." Only by faith can we see the ultimate harvest and hear the shout of the multitudes redeemed through literature.

Regardless of how man may regard us, we must remember Heaven's evaluation of our calling: "There is no higher work than evangelistic canvassing."—*Colporteur Ministry*, p. 12. Nothing is more important in the eyes of God. We are heaven's MVPs. And we can remain such by playing close to our Captain's side. Let us resolve through His power to fully reveal unselfish motivation, true kindness and humility, and faithful perseverance in the face of obstacles.

Invincible Determination

Have you ever faced up to the real reason why you do not have greater success? If you could express your chief lack in just one word or one sentence, what do you think it would be? Most honest literature evangelists would point to the same culprit—a lack of real determination.

Weekly reports indicate that many literature evangelists do not work toward a predetermined daily demonstrations goal. Their demonstrations fluctuate according to the number of leads received. Thus many capable workers hold themselves down in the rut of limited success. If we wish to climb higher, we will have to look to the example of the Master Worker.

Jesus determined *what* He would do for man, and all the powers of hell could not stop Him. Consider His determined will when He "Stedfastly set his face to go to Jerusalem" (Luke 9:51). As Isaiah predicted, in spite of the flogging, the shame, and the spitting, our Example could testify, "No insult can wound me. I have set my face like flint" (Isa. 50:7, N.E.B.).* Because He refused to give in to a weakened human nature, we don't have to give in. In place of our own weak will, we may have His strength and infinite power; in place of our timidity, His boldness and courage. Our faces, too, may become strong as stone. We can refuse to be wounded by insults or to be satisfied with halfway achievements.

One successful literature evangelist told me how he resisted his own inclinations to delay his start for the day. "I knew that the angels were waiting, and that the people were waiting, and that it was *not* the Lord urging me to stay and

* From *The New English Bible*. © The Delegates of the Oxford University Press and the Syndics of the Cambridge University Press 1961, 1970. Reprinted by permission.

pray comfortably at home for another half hour." He recognized that nothing takes the place of earnest work and determined effort.

At times Ellen White had to help the brethren realize that the *business* to be conducted was just as sacred as prayer. She spoke out against lazy workers. "Through persevering exertion they may rise to almost any degree of eminence as Christians, as men of power and influence. But many will never attain superior rank in the pulpit or in business because of their unfixedness of purpose and the laxness of habits."—*Testimonies*, vol. 4, p. 411. Others signally failed because "they have taken things as leisurely as though they had a temporal millennium in which to work for the salvation of souls."—*Ibid.*, p. 413.

What vital quality can lift us above the comfortable level of the status quo? Sir Thomas Buxton summed it up this way: "The longer I live the more I am certain that the great difference between men, between the feeble and the powerful, between the great and the insignificant, is energy, invincible determination of purpose once fixed, and then death or victory."

It is time for us to allow the divine Physician to cut a little of the flab and laxness out of our lives. We must let Him remove the most crippling bunion on the foot of colporteur progress—being satisfied with only three-to-five demo days. Let us work as energetically as He worked to save mankind—and with the same fixed, invincible determination!

"I Fight to Win"

We cannot misunderstand Paul's fighting words. Like hard punches, they strike the soft spots in our lives to toughen us up for the conflicts ahead. In 1 Corinthians 9:26, 27, Paul describes his resolve—the same kind of discipline that should permeate the life of a converted literature evangelist. "I run straight to the goal with purpose in every step. I fight to win. I'm not just shadow-boxing or playing around. Like an athlete I punish my body, treating it roughly, training it to do what it should, not what it wants to" (T.L.B.).*

Literature evangelism does not take us onto a parade ground. It takes us to a real battlefield where we must grapple with a determined enemy for the souls of men. We are not just sparring with an imaginary opponent. All the hosts of hell battle to turn us back.

"Time is short; the enemy will make every effort to magnify in our minds matters of lesser consequence, and to lead us to regard lightly the very work that most needs to be done."—*Colporteur Ministry*, p. 38. Through our selfish natures he will tempt us to seek the easier, less strenuous tasks. He would divert us to anything that will accomplish less than circulating the powerful printed page—"the very work that most needs to be done."

Like the rugged climb on a narrow mountain trail, this work "requires men who are more than weaklings. Men of stamina are wanted, men who will not wait to have their way smoothed and every obstacle removed, . . . men whose . . . hands are strong to do their Master's work. . . . [It requires] an indomitableness that cannot be molded or subdued by

* Verses marked T.L.B. are taken from *The Living Bible*, copyright 1971 by Tyndale House Publishers, Wheaton, Ill. Used by permission.

adverse circumstances."—*The Ministry of Healing*, pp. 497, 498.

These traits characterized the undaunted Paul. He had allowed Jesus to purge his soul of everything negative, hesitant, or selfish. He could run straight for the goal. Every determined tread echoed the divine purpose in his soul. "Instead of following inclination, he did God's will, however crucifying to his own nature."—*Testimonies*, vol. 8, p. 313.

Paul did not "fight as the pugilist practices prior to the fray, beating the air with empty blows, having no opponent. But as, when in actual conflict, he contends for the mastery, overcomes his antagonist by repeated and well-directed blows, beats him to the ground, and holds him there till he acknowledges himself conquered, so did the apostle fight against the temptations of Satan and the evil propensities of the carnal nature."—*Sketches From the Life of Paul*, p. 167.

It sounds almost brutal, doesn't it? But our selfish natures can't be conquered with less severe tactics. "In our own strength it is impossible for us to deny the clamors of our fallen nature."—*The Desire of Ages*, p. 122. Only through Jesus can our old selfish nature be completely crucified. Only in His might can we beat it to the ground and hold it there.

"Pride and self-esteem cannot flourish in the hearts that keep fresh in memory the scenes of Calvary."—*Testimonies*, vol. 2, p. 212. Like Paul, we must keep looking to the cross. Then we will have the stamina, the strong hands, the warm hearts, and the "fight to win."

Above Infirmities

Sunnyside at Avondale College, Cooranbong, Australia! What a privilege I had to walk through this modest dwelling where Ellen G. White lived. I paused before a tiny five-foot-by-seven-foot cubicle, furnished with a single chair. At times, according to the guide, Ellen White would go into this little room to meditate and be alone with God.

Outside I stood by the nearby marker that designates the place of the "miracle furrow." Here Ellen White's dream was fulfilled when the brethren from Iowa misjudged the fruitful soil. All reminded me that God Himself had established the work and that it remains strong in Australia today because God's people heeded His messenger's counsel.

I couldn't help thinking of all that God accomplished in spite of the frailty of the human vessel. When called to Australia, Ellen White had nearly reached the normal age for retirement. She celebrated her sixty-fourth birthday aboard ship en route to Sydney. Her first year "down under" was extremely painful and trying. She described it thus: "Not long after going to Australia, I was stricken with disease. . . . I suffered an attack of inflammatory rheumatism, which prostrated me for eleven months. At times I was in intense agony. . . . But in spite of this I did not cease my work. My right arm, from the elbow to the finger tips, was free from pain; the rest of the arm, the whole of the left arm, and both shoulders, could not be moved voluntarily. A framework was devised, and by the aid of this, I could write. During these eleven months, I wrote twenty-five hundred pages of letter paper."—*Selected Messages*, book 1, p. 104.

In a letter written to the General Conference in 1892 she testified, "Never once has that right hand failed me. My arm and shoulder have been full of suffering, hard to bear, but the hand has been able to hold the pen and trace words that have come to me from the Spirit of the Lord."—*Life Sketches*, p. 340. Despite her intense suffering and the handicap of years, Ellen White produced in Australia masterpieces of Christian literature—*The Desire of Ages, Thoughts From the Mount of Blessing*, and *Christ Our Saviour*.

Most widows suffering such hardship alone in a foreign land would have turned back. Responsible committees today would recommend a permanent return for missionaries so seriously afflicted. But Ellen White in her weakness trusted in the Saviour's might. " 'Sometimes when I felt unable to fill my appointment, I would say. "In faith I will place myself before the people"; and when I did this, strength was given to me to rise above my infirmities, and to bear the message the Lord had given me.' "—*Ibid.*, p. 343.

Someone with less stamina and character than William Arnold would also have turned back.But after six hard weeks without selling a single volume, he kept on placing himself "before the people." He prayed earnestly, and the Lord gave him strength to surmount the obstacles.

Stalwart Henry Thompson, New Zealand's great literature evangelist soul winner, could have put the briefcase on the shelf when he retired. But at 70 years of age and in spite of illness he still placed himself, with the help of his motorbike, "before the people."

When we feel tempted to look back or turn aside from the path of duty, we should remember Ellen White, William Arnold, and Henry Thompson. We should firmly resolve to place ourselves "before the people." As surely as we do this, God will give us strength to bear His message and to rise above infirmities.

Five or Six Times

Perhaps King Joash was thinking of miracles as he wept over the dying prophet Elisha. To him the prophet symbolized God's mighty miracle-working power in behalf of Israel. "O my father, my father, the chariot of Israel, and the horsemen thereof," he wailed (2 Kings 13:14). Would miraculous power die with the prophet? Could Elisha, even from his deathbed, perform just one more miracle for Israel?

Responding to the youthful king's need, Elisha commanded him to "take bow and arrows." Then placing his wrinkled, feeble hands over Joash's smooth, healthy hands, Elisha bade him shoot an arrow eastward through the open window. As it sped toward the captive cities beyond Jordan, Elisha confidently cried, "The arrow of the Lord's deliverance" (verse 17).

Then Elisha demonstrated to King Joash how God works miracles for His people. "Take the arrows," commanded the prophet. "Smite upon the ground" (verse 18). Without much enthusiasm or strength, Joash struck the ground three times. In dismay and disappointment Elisha exclaimed, "Thou shouldest have smitten five or six times" (verse 19). If he had, he would have overthrown the Syrians, but now he could achieve only partial victory.

I believe Ellen White's comment on Joash's experience especially applies to literature evangelists. "When God opens the way for the accomplishment of a certain work and gives assurance of success, the chosen instrumentality must do all in his power to bring about the promised result. In proportion to the enthusiasm and perseverance with which the work is carried forward will be the success given. *God can work miracles for His people only as they act their part with untiring energy.*"—*Prophets and Kings*, p. 263. (Italics supplied.)

God can work miracles for you and me today, but only when we do our part with untiring energy, enthusiasm, and perseverance. It all depends on how many times we "smite upon the ground." We won't see many miracles after only three or four blows, but let us try five or six times and see what happens! We must not stop after just three or four attempts to close a sale. We must try five or six times, and then we will see some miraculous decisions. We must not rest satisfied with just three or four calls each morning, afternoon, and evening. We must give five or six demonstrations and then watch God work miracles.

Put this miracle rule to the test. Check the average number of exhibitions you have made during the past six weeks. Then every week for the next six weeks "smite five or six times" for every three canvasses you gave previously. Which would you prefer—three tries without miracles or five or six with miracles?

Section Four

Surrender Self, Duty First

The Tilt of the Mirror
A Ministry Like His
Give Yourself Up
Where the Coward Ends
Simplify Your Life
The Little Foxes
When Will It Come?

The Tilt of the Mirror

In the book *In His Image*, William Jennings Bryan wrote about the responses a speaker elicits from his hearers. He contrasted the people's reactions to the Greek Demosthenes and to the Roman Cicero. Both men were capable leaders, orators, and statesmen. But an important distinction marked the two. " 'When Cicero spake the people said, "How well Cicero speaks"; when Demosthenes spake his hearers cried, "Let us go against Philip." ' "—Page 252. Both apparently won that which they wanted most. Cicero won applause and attracted men to his own brilliance, but Demosthenes inspired men to action—to fight for his cause.

After twenty and more centuries, we still have both types of men and women. The Cicero-type are apparent everywhere. They constantly thrust themselves into the limelight. Their suggestions are always calculated to show their brilliance. They have plenty of ideas—sparks of their own kindling—but do little really solid, practical work. Many followers find the glitter attractive, but they don't stay very long or achieve very much. However, the Demosthenes-type are different. They do not push themselves forward and are, therefore, not quite so obvious. A deep inner conviction and an earnest sense of duty motivate them. When they speak, others are moved to action—to give of their lives because they have seen a great cause rather than a merely clever person.

During a visit to a village in Uganda I met a young lad with *five* mirrors on the handlebars of his new bicycle. His bright smile seemed to match all the *maradadi* (Swahili for "shiny extras"). When I examined the mirrors, I discovered that each reflected the rider's face! Thus he could watch himself from all angles as he pedaled along in all his glory!

We chuckle at this lad's ego, but don't we often attract a little too much attention to self? Cicero-like we focus the mirrors of life on ourselves. We need a divine hand to tilt them upward, enabling us to behold the glory of Christ's self-sacrificing love. Then our service will become less Cicero-like and more Demosthenes-like—as Teddy Roosevelt put it, "Less shouting, more shooting!"

In New Testament times what moved the multitudes to the Jordan to listen to John the Baptist? What about his preaching brought a whole nation to repentance and made Satan fear for the very safety of his kingdom? "He sought not to attract men to himself, but to lift their thoughts higher and still higher, until they should rest upon the Lamb of God."—*The Desire of Ages*, p. 179.

"John was great in the sight of the Lord, when, before the messengers from the Sanhedrin, before the people, and before his own disciples, he refrained from seeking honor for himself, but pointed all to Jesus as the Promised One."—*Ibid.*, p. 219.

What about your service and mine? Do we inspire the people we contact to think of how clever and able we are? Or do we lift them higher and still higher to the Lamb of God and His great cause for mankind? It all depends on the tilt of the mirror. Shall we let Jesus reposition ours? Then, like John (and Demosthenes), we will move thousands to fight for our King!

A Ministry Like His

Nearly 140 years has elapsed since Jesus entered the Most Holy Place to complete His ministry for man. We have already gone nearly two decades beyond the probationary time God granted the generation of Noah. We must take time for earnest evaluation. Why haven't we achieved more? Why do we experience so little Pentecostal power? What do we really need in our lives to enable us to serve as He ministered?

These questions strike the sensitive nerves of the conscience, and we feel compelled to confess we have not yet made the commitment that He wants us to make. We are not yet willing to discipline and sacrifice self as He did. Pride and selfishness still pollute our service. The graph of our successes and failures has moved up and down in a way similar to the record of the sons of thunder before their conversion. We have manifested much finite ignorance and weakness and little infinite wisdom and might.

Yet, two qualities illuminated Jesus' every act—two secrets of His power by which our ministry might become like His.

Duty to God's work always came first in His life. As a young lad He asserted, "I must be about my Father's business" (Luke 2:49). After meeting the needs of a hungry soul, He reminded His disciples, "My meat is to do the will of him that sent me, and to finish his work" (John 4:34). Jesus had no higher priorities than the work of God. "Christ brought His desires and wishes into strict abeyance to His mission—the mission that bore the insignia of Heaven. He made everything subordinate to the work that He came to this world to accomplish."—*Gospel Workers*, p. 111.

His service was completely devoid of self. Satan claimed

that no being could lead a completely selfless life. Jesus' beautiful earthly ministry disproved this claim. His entire life was wholly centered in helping and blessing others. "He . . . made them feel the completeness of His identification with their interests and happiness."—*Evangelism*, p. 148. "It will be seen that the glory shining in the face of Jesus is the glory of self-sacrificing love."—*The Desire of Ages*, p. 20. And in our service today "no other influence that can surround the human soul has such power as the influence of an unselfish life" (*The Ministry of Healing*, p. 470).

The same two great qualities will characterize the lives of God's workers. They will subordinate everything to His work. Life will glow with the glory of a selfless service to man. But we must remember that "we are not to try to do the work of the potter. Our part is to yield ourselves to be molded by the Master Worker."—*Ibid*., p. 472.

When this happens, our ministry will resemble His.

Give Yourself Up

"Let canvassing evangelists give themselves up to be worked by the Holy Spirit. Let them by persevering prayer take hold of the power which comes from God."—*Colporteur Ministry*, p. 106.

Have you ever given yourself up entirely to the control of the Spirit for a full day or an entire week? What happens when a literature evangelist completely abandons selfish desires and lets the Holy Spirit take charge? I believe three differences will show up in the life of such a worker.

First of all, he will have a much stronger soul-winning ministry. Selfish eagerness for commissions and benefits will never be manifested. The Spirit-controlled literature evangelist will have only one burning desire: to deliver God's last message and to make one more soul ready for His kingdom. He will not feel content to sell children's sets or health sets alone. He would rather sell a *Triumph of God's Love* than $1,000 worth without the important decision books. When the Spirit takes charge, he will enroll more in Bible correspondence courses, pray with more people, and return to more customers' homes for Bible studies. Dozens will be baptized where now there is one.

Second, a holy boldness, a confident fearlessness, will take possession of his life. He will not hesitate to speak to anyone anywhere about God's books. Like John the Baptist, "unawed by the human, because he had looked upon the Divine," he will stand "erect and fearless" before all men, "because he had bowed low before the King" (*The Desire of Ages*, p. 103).

During a recent Big Week when I really let the Holy Spirit take charge, I often felt surprised by my lack of the usual fear and hesitation. I sold books at times and places where ordinarily I would have felt reticent. God's Spirit seemed to urge me forward as He did Philip when he ran beside the chariot of the Ethiopian treasurer and cried out, "Understandest thou what thou readest?" (Acts 8:30).

For instance, an inner voice prompted me to stop and go back to speak with a young couple examining the markers in an old country cemetery. I spoke kindly to them about my hope in Christ and what the book *The Desire of Ages* meant to me. In a few minutes the young lady was urging her rather bewildered fiancé to pay me cash for this priceless treasure. It was my first sale in a cemetery!

Again the Spirit prompted me to approach a well-lighted

doorway about 10:00 p.m. A friendly young married man confessed that he had not opened the Bible or attended church since his boyhood. What a joy to satisfy his heart's hunger with *The Bible Story*, *Triumph of God's Love*, and *The Desire of Ages!*

Yes, when God's Spirit takes charge, a fearless confidence will possess the worker. He will not hesitate to speak to anyone anywhere!

Third, a literature worker yielded to the Spirit's control will refuse to look back. A new sense of urgency will control his daily program. He will solemnly recognize that the judgment hour cannot linger much longer. With joy and a holy enthusiasm he will labor beyond his normal hours without becoming tired or weary. There will be no selfish thought of a more remunerative job. Time and material things will soon be no longer. He will stay on and finish God's work.

Yes, all this will happen in your life when you let the Holy Spirit take charge. With a new boldness you will circulate the books. You will never falter or turn to less important work. Others will observe your steadfastness and joy and will feel compelled to leave their ordinary occupations to join you on the front lines. Thousands will be converted, as on the day of Pentecost.

Would you like to see it happen? Are you willing to give yourself up to be worked by the Holy Spirit?

Where the Coward Ends

I will never forget Elder A. W. Staples' vivid word picture of his first day in the literature ministry. At that time in South Africa the colporteur started alone, with a single prospectus. When young Staples reached his territory, he circled the block several times as he tried to postpone that dreaded first-door moment. He described his experience in these words: "I took myself firmly by the throat and declared, 'Staples, this is where the coward ends and the man begins!' I turned in at the next gate and marched myself up to that first home." Discipline and duty had won out. And Elder Staples became a strong worker and later an outstanding evangelist and conference and union president.

We who battle the enemy on the front lines every day understand such a struggle. We make that choice every hour, all through the week. Our cowardly, selfish inclinations point one way, the noble pursuit of duty the other. And in between calls, the enemy makes "every effort to magnify in our minds matters of lesser consequence, and to lead us to regard lightly the very work that most needs to be done" (*Colporteur Ministry*, p. 38). He works through our fallen nature, enticing us to pamper self, to choose the easier task, and to keep us sidetracked with matters of lesser consequence.

But when God's Spirit takes charge, He helps us put first things first and hourly crucify our selfish inclinations. All the energies of our lives focus on getting the message into more homes—the very work God wants most to accomplish. We understand that "the Lord requires us to obey the voice of duty, when there are other voices all around us urging us to pursue an opposite course. . . . We must resist and conquer inclination, and obey the voice of conscience without parleying or compromise."—*Testimonies*, vol. 5, p. 69.

The same attitude has distinguished the great achievers for God through all time. Amid the clamor of a thousand voices of inclination they heard and obeyed the still, small voice of duty. This was Joseph's experience. "In his early years he had consulted duty rather than inclination."—*Patriarchs and Prophets*, p. 222. It was the same with Paul. "Instead of following inclination, he did God's will, however crucifying to his own nature."—*Testimonies*, vol. 8, p. 313. And duty always came first with the Master Himself. "My meat," He asserted, "is to do the will of him that sent me, and to finish his work" (John 4:34). Read *The Desire of Ages*, page 759. No matter how mercilessly the storm of Satan's wrath beat upon Jesus, he could not discourage Him or *drive* Him from the work He came to do.

Proverbs 24:27 can picture the wise literature worker's program: "Prepare thy work without, and make it fit for thyself in the field; and afterwards build thine house." "No earthly ties," Ellen White counsels, "no earthly considerations, should weigh one moment in the scale against duty to the cause and work of God."—*Testimonies*, vol. 3, p. 500.

We must keep looking to the cross and keep on crucifying these natural inclinations. We must let the voice of duty overrule. We must never allow the things of this world, no matters of lesser consequence, to come before the work God wants most to have done. Every moment we will let the coward die and let the *real* man and woman shine through.

Simplify Your Life

Joseph Fort Newton complained of the "tedious egotism of our day . . . when men are self-centered and self-obsessed, unable to get themselves off their hands." Thomas Carlyle spoke of the ubiquitous "black spot in our sunshine, the shadow of ourselves." Ellen White talked about the same problem: "We carry around with us a bundle of self that we regard as altogether too precious to be given up."—*Testimonies,* vol. 9, p. 189. And most of us have learned through shameful experience that the more we let self rule, the more difficult and complicated life becomes.

Dean W. R. Inge aptly contrasts the two kinds of lives: "He who will live for himself shall have small troubles, but they will seem to him great. He who will live for others shall have great troubles, but they shall seem to him small."

The same two types of people are evident among Adventist workers. Some people devote considerable energy to making themselves look good. Personal ambition drives them, filling their lives with tension and complications. Their lives seem weighted down with burdens and problems. On the other hand, the workers whose hearts center wholly in Christ and in others exude a spirit of unharried serenity. Life to them is uncluttered and uncomplicated. By glorifying Him and not self in every contact they remove the black spot of self from the sunshine of their lives.

Customers quickly recognize the difference, and sometimes they write in to tell us about it. In one recent letter a prospect complained that the representative refused to allow her to buy a single copy of *The Desire of Ages.* He insisted that she must buy the entire Bible Reference Library. The customer felt that such fine Christian publications should be represented with a different spirit. So she requested that someone else call, because she really wanted to buy *The Desire of Ages*. Unfortunately, that literature evangelist left her home with both a heavy bundle of self and a too-heavy briefcase. He left behind a dark shadow of self.

Another customer wrote our HHES office to commend a literature evangelist. She told how Mr.——— took an interest in each of her three lively children, was careful to get their first names correct, and showed concern regarding her husband's work and her job as an elementary teacher. She concluded her letter: "We have had many salesmen come to our home, but never before one who had such great empathy and ability. He was interesting, truthful, courteous, and humble. We feel our lives have been made richer for having made his acquaintance, and we felt you might be pleased to learn how well he represented your company." You may be sure he left that home with a happy heart and a light briefcase, leaving behind only the sunshine of Christ's presence and some truth-filled books.

"If pride and selfishness were laid aside, five minutes would remove most difficulties."—*Early Writings*, p. 119. Let us each take those five minutes every morning and allow the Master to lift off our bundles of self.

The Little Foxes

"Why don't we consider Bob K——— ?" a committee member suggests enthusiastically. "He's hardworking and dedicated, is near the top in sales, and has a fine wife to back him up. He deserves an opportunity."

"Yes, he is a nice fellow," another more seasoned leader agrees, "but he's too——" And the committee turns to the next name on the board.

Because this great literature program depends so much on the right leader, church administrators are constantly watching literature evangelists and evaluating them in terms of leadership possibilities. And just a little too much this or that may keep an otherwise deserving worker from receiving a call to larger responsibilities. I have jotted down seven questionable characteristics that I have heard leaders point out on various committees. They are the "little foxes" that spoil the developing vine of an otherwise qualified candidate for leadership assignments.

1. **Too negative**—He is probably intelligent, well organized, and fairly successful. But someone heard him talking in a negative way—the work or the territory was difficult, the prices were too high, and so on.

2. **Too snag conscious**—This person sees the obstacles instead of opportunities. There is always some reason why a good plan won't work.

3. **Too demanding**—Such an individual has PR problems. He hasn't learned how to sell others on his program. He expects the leaders he works with to give him everything he wants, and he gets angry if they don't.

4. **Too critical**—He revels in passing on unsavory bits, particularly about those who supervise the work. His favorite

preface is "Have you heard about Elder ———?" Loyalty is not in his lexicon.

5. **Too eager for position—**By pulling strings and polishing apples he constantly primes the "call" pump. He makes phone calls and gets his friends to make phone calls in his behalf. He has forgotten that the Lord places the burden on "the brethren who have tested him" and not just on his own heart.

6. **Too unreliable—**While he is willing to do something big and important, he neglects the little duties that are assigned. He looks fairly bright in the limelight, but the luster fades when he is asked to help with less dramatic offstage duties.

7. **Too satisfied—**Such a person feels content with mediocre achievements. He shies away from higher goals. After all, he *is* working pretty hard to accomplish *all* he is accomplishing now. And it is nice to be home a few more days or a few more evenings with the family.

Could it be that just one of these "little foxes" has kept your vine from climbing and bearing all the fruit that it is possible to bear? Let's check up on ourselves and make sure we are the kind of men and women God (and the brethren) can trust with more responsibilities.

When Will It Come?

Conditions in both the world and the church declare that we teeter on the verge of the final crisis. The predicted moral, economic, and political catastrophes are rapidly coming to a climax. Surely our God will not wait much longer for the final outpouring of His Spirit!

"But," you say, "we have been preaching the judgment-hour message for one hundred forty years. Why haven't we received His power in all its fullness?" *The Desire of Ages*, page 672, explains why: "They do not surrender the soul to be guided and controlled by the divine agencies. We cannot use the Holy Spirit. The Spirit is to use us. . . . But many will not submit to this. They want to manage themselves. This is why they do not receive the heavenly gift." Our big obstacle, then, is our refusal to surrender the will. We want to control our own lives.

George Whitefield described the difficulty of conquering and subduing the monster of self. " 'O for further leadings into the chambers of that selfish, sensual, and devilish imagery, that yet lie latent in my partly renewed heart! This self-love, what a *Proteus!* This self-will, what a *Hydra*! This remaining body of sin and death, what an *Antichrist!* what a scarlet whore! what a hell! what a red dragon! what a cursed monster is it! How hard, how slow, he dies!' "—Ruth Gordon Short, *George Whitefield, Trumpet of the Lord*, pp. 108, 109. That is the real problem, isn't it? The old man, the cursed monster of self, elbows the Holy Spirit aside. The heavenly Guest politely stands by. He takes control only as we invite Him.

Ellen White reveals how we can turn over our lives to the Holy Spirit's control. "Let canvassing evangelists give themselves up to be worked by the Holy Spirit. Let them by persevering prayer take hold of the power which comes from God."—*Colporteur Ministry*, p. 106. When we do this, we will experience new success and new power. A new boldness, a new zeal, will take possession of our lives. We will not be afraid or hesitant to go to any door. Our great objective will be to get souls ready for heaven.

When will the latter rain fall? How can we have it without measure in our lives. "To Jesus, who emptied Himself for the salvation of lost humanity, the Holy Spirit was given without measure. So it will be given to every follower of Christ when the whole heart is surrendered for His indwelling."—*Thoughts From the Mount of Blessing*, p. 21.

Some years ago a DC-6 plane was flying high above Colorado's Rockies on its nonstop flight from San Francisco to Chicago. Suddenly the propeller on the right inboard engine spun loose from its mount. With a thunderous bang it crashed through the upper fuselage. A subzero gale and bits of wreckage assailed the passengers. While the pilot worked furiously at the controls, the stewardess bravely announced, "Fasten your seat belts. We'll be in Denver in twenty minutes."

As the plane lost altitude, passengers anxiously prayed. One fainted. Another slumped forward, dead of a heart attack. Relief overwhelmed them when the plane touched down safely. The pilot said later, "In a situation like that you just move over a little bit and let God take over."

Literature workers, we are all hurtling rapidly toward this world's last great crisis. The people in our territory look to us to pilot them safely to God's kingdom. Isn't it time to move over and let the Holy Spirit take complete control?

Section Five

A More Positive Attitude

Tongue Power
The Battles of the Lord
Remedy the Negative
Focus on Power
Helpstones of the Eternal

Tongue Power

"No matter how low I feel," a first-year worker testified, "Brother ——— knows just what to say to lift me up! He talks about the possibilities and success and makes me believe I can make it!" Brother ——— possessed a talent for instilling enthusiasm and courage in others. The aura that surrounded him sparkled with hope and confidence. Alive and vibrant with faith, he marched forward to his highest year in sales and souls.

"Even when my courage is high," a solid career literature evangelist observed, "I start feeling low just listening to Brother ———. He's always harping about the difficulties—seems to have a sort of cancellation syndrome. He complains about the HHES and criticizes his leaders." A far different spirit permeated the atmosphere of this colporteur's life. His words had a dulling and blighting effect. Both his sales and his soul-winning records trailed embarrassingly behind the other workers in the conference.

King Solomon aptly said, "Death and life are in the power of the tongue" (Prov. 18:21). One worker's sour tongue, coated with a critical spirit, spews out an atmosphere of blight and death. Another worker's tongue, inspired by love, breathes out courage and life. The one tongue hasn't yet been crucified with Christ. It isn't prompted by the positive principles of true Christianity. The other speaks as Christ's tongue would speak: "I am come that they might have life, and that they might have it more abundantly" (John 10:10).

How we need to guard our words, speaking only that which brings hope and encouragement to our fellow workers! Note well Ellen White's words regarding sanctified tongue power: "Cultivate the habit of speaking well of others. Dwell upon the good qualities of those with whom you associate, and see as little as possible of their errors and failings. When tempted to complain of what someone has said or done, praise something in that person's life or character. . . . Earnest workers have no time for dwelling upon the faults of others. We cannot afford to live on the husks of others' faults or failings. . . . Too often we forget that our fellow laborers are in need of strength and cheer. Take care to assure them of your interest and sympathy. Help them by your prayers, and let them know that you do it."—*The Ministry of Healing*, pp. 492, 493.

Let us each resolve today to live on a higher plane—above the husks of others' faults. We must resist the evil one's daily attempts to get us bogged down with critical minutiae. Let us dedicate our tongues to lifting the lives of all within the circle of our influence. We should dwell on the good qualities of others. We can look for something praiseworthy in their lives. We can give others strength and cheer. We can assure them of our interest and sympathy. Hope and confidence or death and discouragement may be determined by the power of the tongue. Let us make sure that our every word savors of life unto life.

The Battles of the Lord

David and his men were on their way to battle. Filled with indignation, they intended to punish the man who had insulted them. And surely it seemed that they had just cause for retaliation. As fugitives in the wilderness of Paran, David's band had protected the flocks of the wealthy Nabal, a descendant of Caleb. But when they had asked for supplies to relieve their necessities, Nabal insultingly replied, "Who is David?"

A man with such a stingy spirit surely deserved punishment. After all, Samuel had anointed David to rule Israel. Surely *he* had a right to put the insolent Nabal in his place. Fortunately, God had other plans and spoke to David through the kindly acts and words of Nabal's wife, Abigail. This godly woman's sweet spirit soothed David's irritated feelings. Listen to her beautiful appeal: "My lord fighteth the battles of the Lord, and evil hath not been found in thee all thy days" (1 Sam. 25:28). Abigail implied that David was stooping to something beneath his nobility. God's man ought to direct his energies toward higher, more important tasks. "He should fight the battles of the Lord. He was not to seek revenge for personal wrongs, even though persecuted as a traitor."—*Patriarchs and Prophets*, p. 666. David humbly received Abigail's rebuke and blessed her for turning him back from shedding blood.

Sometimes God's literature workers today feel tempted to react like David did to human smallness or accusations. Satan stirs up feelings of resentment and goads us to nurture petty grudges and desires for revenge. He wants us to reflect his own rebellious nature. He delights in keeping us fussing over unimportant, selfish little issues.

But as Abigail reminded David, we have something larger to attend to. The big task is the battle of the Lord—defending His character and His law against the onslaughts of Satan's forces. We dare not allow ourselves to be diverted to fight petty personal battles. As one unknown writer so aptly warns, "Don't stop to stone the devil's dogs . . . or chase the devil's rabbits. . . . God has never bidden you to defend your character!" When we keep our guns aimed at the old roaring lion himself, we are not going to be diverted by a mosquito bite or even a bumblebee sting. We've got big battles to fight—the battles of the Lord!

Let us therefore keep our swords, our energies, and our words aimed in the right direction. Then neither the hosts of hell nor the taunts of a thousand Nabals shall ever prevail against us or divert us to start battling for ourselves. The Lord needs individuals now to fight some mighty battles for the finishing of His work. Let's fight them the way the godly Abigail and the noble King David recommended!

Remedy the Negative

"I could leave them money when I die. But they would just fight over it. I want to leave them something that will do them some good in life." Thus a well-to-do grandmother in Wichita, Kansas, explained why she was ordering 14 sets of *The Bible Story* for her grandchildren!

Our literature worker's heart beat excitedly when he called back to deliver those sets and pick up the check—the biggest he had ever anticipated. But after the maid had ushered him inside, this dear old lady blurted out, "Mr. ———, I have changed my mind about that order." Gamely attempting to muster a smile, the bookman waited in near agony for her explanation.

At such a horrible, torturous moment I am sure most of us could not resist thoughts of fear and despair. Our natural, finite minds, after millenniums of sin and death, almost automatically expect the worst to happen. So our brother in Wichita mentally winced in anticipation of the blow as this good grandmother continued. "I was thinking last night that I really ought to get a set of these *Bible Story* books for myself. So could you change that order to fifteen instead of fourteen sets?"

When these miracle sales happen, should servants of a miracle-working God be surprised? Shouldn't the love of Christ so conquer our lower, negative nature that we will *expect* great and miraculous things? But we must keep constantly on guard. Almost every day in our experience the old, natural, negative man will attempt to rear his ugly head. God's messenger gives some very precise counsel on how to beat him down, on how to remedy the negative.

First, we should avoid any expression of negative thoughts. The reason for this is clear: "Satan cannot read our thoughts, but he can see our actions, hear our words; and from his long knowledge of the human family, he can shape his temptations to take advantage of our weak points of character. And how often do we let him into the secret of how he may obtain the victory over us."—*Messages to Young People*, p. 328. One negative thought expressed encourages Satan to add a hundred more and thus bring gloom and despondency to our souls. If a negative thought comes, let us never let him know about it. Let us never give him the satisfaction that he can darken our countenances or sadden our lives.

Second, we must cultivate thankfulness and a spirit of

praise. "That which at first seems difficult, by constant repetition grows easy, until right thoughts and actions become habitual. . . . When tempted to complain of what someone has said or done, praise something in that person's life or character. Cultivate thankfulness. Praise God for His wonderful love in giving Christ to die for us. It never pays to think of our grievances. God calls upon us to think of His mercy and His matchless love, that we may be inspired with praise."—*The Ministry of Healing*, pp. 491, 492. Like sin and righteousness, the positive and the negative do not mix. It is just not possible to complain while we are praising God or talking about the good qualities of our fellow workers.

Focus on Power

Dr. Brownsberger smiled as he checked the fit on my first pair of glasses. "OK, Joe, now take a look outside."

"Wow!" I almost went into orbit. "Everything is so much sharper, so much more beautiful," I replied.

Those corrective lenses opened up an amazing new world to my nearsighted eyes. I had squinted and strained my eyes for several years because I didn't want to wear glasses, but now I wondered why I had waited so long. Those distant objects were no longer blurred. Even Bonnie's smile from the other side of the academy dining hall looked brighter and more beautiful!

And isn't it strange how we, likewise, hold back when God tries to improve our mental and spiritual vision? Nearsightedly, we focus on our own earthly weaknesses, problems, and sins, and thus we blur the higher heavenly image of God's power, love, and purity. The cure for our spiritual myopia comes only through looking to Jesus. As we behold Him, constantly seeing His mighty power and perfect love, the corrective lenses are applied. Our vision becomes clear. We discover a new world. That which lies ahead becomes bright and beautiful.

God's messenger talks of this need in *Testimonies*, volume 5, page 741: "Many fix their eyes upon the terrible wickedness existing around them, the apostasy and weakness on every side, and they talk of these things until their hearts are filled with sadness and doubt. They keep uppermost before the mind the masterly working of the archdeceiver and dwell upon the discouraging features of their experience, while they seem to lose sight of the heavenly Father's power and His matchless love. All this is as Satan would have it. It is a mistake to think of the enemy of righteousness as clothed with so great power, when we dwell so little upon the love of God and His might. We must talk of the mightiness of Christ. . . . The Son of the Highest has strength to fight the battle for us, and 'through Him that loved us' we may come off 'more than conquerors.' . . . He has power to dispel the dark shadows which Satan casts across our path; and, in place of darkness and discouragement, the sunlight of His glory shines into our hearts."

"Then let us not gather together all the unpleasant pictures—the iniquities and corruptions and disappointments, the evidences of Satan's power—to hang in the halls of our memory, to talk over and mourn over until our souls are filled with discouragement. . . . There are, thank God, brighter and more cheering pictures which the Lord has presented to us. Let us group together the blessed assurances of His love as precious treasures, that we may look upon them continually."—*Ibid.*, pp. 744, 745.

God forbid that we should dwell on the power of a defeated foe! We are marching at the command of One who has never lost a battle. All the forces of the infinite Creator of the universe have been pledged to give us victory and success. As we keep focusing on this power our service will vibrate with the energy of heaven.

Helpstones of the Eternal

Israel had gathered in Mizpah at Samuel's call for revival. Mistaking the convocation for a threat of war, the Philistines marshaled their forces to attack the assembled Israelites. Samuel cried earnestly to the Lord, and God sent great thunder and mighty bolts of lightning that struck down thousands of the idolatrous warriors.

The men of Israel seized their weapons, pursued the Philistines to Beth-car, and completely routed the entire enemy army. And on the very field where 30,000 Israelites had died and the ark had been captured twenty years before, Samuel set up a great stone monument. He called it Ebenezer, or Helpstone. " 'This is witness,' he said, 'that the Eternal has helped us' " (1 Sam. 7:12, Moffatt).*

Ellen White refers to "monumental pillars, reminders of what the Lord has done to comfort us and to save us from the hand of the destroyer" (*Steps to Christ*, p. 125). She urges us to "keep fresh in our memory all the tender mercies that God has shown us—the tears He has wiped away, the pains He has soothed, the anxieties removed, the fears dispelled, the wants

* From *The Bible: A New Translation* by James Moffatt. Copyright by James Moffatt 1954. Used by permission of Harper & Row, Publishers, Incorporated.

supplied, the blessings bestowed" *(ibid.)*.

Why not take a few moments right now to review all that God has done for you recently? Go to your customer file and slowly flip through your weekly contracts. Let them serve as your Ebenezers, monumental pillars that can remind you of the miracles God worked in the homes of your customers. At some homes you had seemed surrounded by the forces of darkness, but because of prayer and tears, God turned defeat into victory. Where there was anger or prejudice or poverty He soothed, overruled, or supplied the unexpected means with which to buy. At times you could almost hear the thunder of the Eternal and see the lightning strike in the right place at the right time.

There was that earnest young couple for whom you arranged Bible studies and who later, at their baptism, thanked you for bringing the books to their door. There was your fellow worker whom you lifted through a sales slump with helpful words and deeds. Feeling the grip of his hand, hearing his "Thank you for caring," and seeing him press forward in the work made it a precious chapter in your life. Then there were the rallies, the institutes, the precious times of fellowship, and the hundreds of blessings and privileges that come in our service for the Master.

"Far more than we do, we need to speak of the precious chapters in our experience."—*Christ's Object Lessons*, p. 338. Why not write down all that looms large in your memory? Let these "monumental pillars" stand out forever as beacon lights of blessings in your soul. Gather your family around and recount the precious episodes. Lift your voice in songs of praise, and let your witness ring clear that to this point in time the Eternal has indeed helped you.

Section Six

A Challenge to Students

To Risk, to Dare
Climbing the Wrong Mountain
What Would Jesus Do?

To Risk, to Dare

Arch Whitman, a young insurance salesman in Halifax, Nova Scotia, took seriously his boss's suggestion that he wasn't aggressive enough. A few moments later he spotted three workmen on a scaffold outside his seventeenth-floor office window. He held up a note that suggested they should have some life, accident, and disability insurance. The workmen indicated that they would talk if Whitman would join them on the scaffold. He had himself lowered by a cable from the roof and sold one man a $50,000 life insurance policy on the spot.

Arch Whitman was willing to risk something in order to insure someone else's life. All great achievers possess some of this venturesome spirit. They are not afraid to take risks in order to reach worthy goals in life. Theodore Roosevelt once said, "No man is worth his salt unless he is ready at all times to risk his life, his health, his well-being in a great cause." *The Desire of Ages* tells us (p. 49) that Christ Himself was willing to risk failure and eternal loss in order to save man.

Years ago God asked me to give up my own plans and risk a summer in literature evangelism. Since I had no father to guarantee my school expenses, it seemed safer to take a definite-wage-per-hour job on an Iowa farm or at the academy broom factory. My teachers seemed worried, and one even thought I would return home in a few weeks' time. A friend refused to be my partner, explaining, "I want to make sure I get back to school next fall.'' But after five summers of wonderful blessings as a student literature evangelist and having finished college debt-free, I learned that God never calls to failure. Whatever we risk for His cause He repays us a hundredfold.

If you are a young person, what are you planning to do for God's great cause this summer? Have you considered becoming a student literature evangelist? Have you thought of what it would mean to God and to the thousands of people who are waiting for these precious books? Have you thought of what it might mean in your own life?

If I had refused to take the risk that first summer, instead of enjoying the thrill of helping direct God's worldwide publishing program I might still be back there trying to raise hogs and corn on an Iowa farm. I know what literature evangelism did for me and for thousands of other students around the world. It can change the entire course of your life. It will fit you for an exciting role in the closing work of the gospel. It can determine your very destiny.

''God is putting burdens upon more inexperienced shoulders. He is fitting them to be care-taking, to venture, to run risks.''—*Life Sketches,* p. 245. I dare you to respond, no matter how inexperienced your shoulders may be. No matter how much money you can make at a secular job, I dare you to change your plans! Ellen White declared that ''young men and young women who should be engaged . . . in the canvassing work should not be bound down to mechanical employment'' *(Colporteur Ministry,* p. 28*)*. I dare you to dedicate your summer to this new, exciting venture. I dare you to run the risk for God, to be a student literature evangelist!

Climbing the Wrong Mountain

One of our great young people's leaders tells the story of the teen-age climbers who set out to scale the highest peak of a certain mountain range. When they returned, one of the young men expressed the feelings of the group: "We had fun, but we climbed the wrong mountain." They had expended tremendous energy, but they had failed to reach any meaningful objective.

Today entirely new mountain ranges of opportunities and knowledge loom on every young person's horizon. Many trails and peaks are beckoning. To discern and choose the best is as difficult as deciding which of Colorado's magnificent pinnacles to climb first. An impulsive choice could lead to disappointment. It is better to follow in the sure footprints of the Guide who knows the way. Christ Himself will lead the trusting student up the right summit, to the heights of skill and knowledge that rank highest in the sight of Heaven.

Inspiration defines clearly the "peaks" that count most with God. The need in His work is not for "great and learned men" or "eloquent sermonizers" (*Gospel Workers*, p. 64). He calls for self-sacrificing young people, youth embued with the practical, saving energy of the Holy Spirit. "The knowledge of the most learned man, if he has not learned in Christ's school, is foolishness so far as leading souls to Christ is concerned."—*Colporteur Ministry*, p. 35. In God's eyes the "greatest of all wisdom" is that which "brings man in touch with men, and enables him to arouse their better nature and inspire them to a higher life" (*Education*, p. 66).

Knowing how to touch and inspire the hearts of others and to win them for Christ's kingdom is the greatest height of wisdom to which a mortal may aspire. And God has clearly marked out the trail to enable thinking youth to reach this summit. It certainly cannot be learned by proxy or through classroom theory and lecture. It develops best by participation, through an intensive experience in door-to-door and one-to-one contacts.

Ellen White declares that an experience in student literature evangelism "may properly be termed higher education" and "the very best education" young people can obtain *(Colporteur Ministry*, pp. 33, 32). It is God's toughening-up process to prepare young men and women for the "hard, earnest, self-sacrificing labor that has to be done in many foreign fields, where the third angel's message must be carried under difficult and trying circumstances" *(Testimonies*, vol. 9, p. 78).

Could the lack of this practical training explain why thousands of Adventist graduates become highly qualified professionally but still feel awkwardly inadequate about knocking on a door and personally leading a soul to Christ? The records of countless dedicated workers throughout the world testify that the more experience they enjoyed in literature evangelism, the more effective their service for God. Will you turn to the less meaningful fun on the lower slopes of the wrong mountains? Or will you let God choose the peak that means the most to Him and that will prepare you best for the tough climbs ahead?

What Would Jesus Do?

"Elder, every spring when I hire some of the top students for our summer camps," one of our best youth leaders recently confided to me, "something troubles me inside. I know what those summers of canvassing did for my life, and I don't like to see these students miss that blessing. Our camping program provides wholesome employment, but we can't give students what they would get in a summer of literature evangelism." ("The very best education young men can obtain is by entering the canvassing field and working from house to house."—*Colporteur Ministry*, p. 32.)

This youth leader's candid concern raises some vital questions. Of all the summer job opportunities for Adventist young people today, which offers the greatest opportunity for service? Which best develops a young person's ability to win souls for Christ? If Jesus Himself were a college student today, what would He choose to do during the summer? Can you picture the One who knows how few summers of probation remain devoting His *entire* summer to touring Europe, working on a construction crew, or backpacking and campfires and surfboarding?

What would Jesus do today? How would He serve? Ellen White pictures it beautifully. "Christ might have occupied the highest place among the teachers of the Jewish nation, but He preferred rather to take the gospel to the poor. He went from place to place, that those in the highways and byways might hear the words of truth. . . .

"Never was there such an evangelist as Christ. He was the Majesty of heaven, but He humbled Himself to take our nature, that He might meet men where they were. . . . Thus He went from city to city, from town to town, preaching the gospel and healing the sick. . . . What a busy life He led! Day by day He might have been seen entering the humble abodes of want and sorrow, speaking hope to the downcast and peace to the distressed. Gracious, tenderhearted, pitiful, He went about lifting up the bowed-down and comforting the sorrowful. Wherever He went, He carried blessing."—*The Ministry of Healing*, pp. 20-24.

Student friend, what better way could you follow in His footsteps this summer than in student literature evangelism? This work provides the opportunities for a ministry like His, to work from town to town, to enter the humble abodes, and to lift up the downcast and distressed.

Regardless of what you have thought of doing this summer, won't you find a quiet retreat somewhere this Sabbath and let Jesus tell you what *He* really wants you to do? Through literature evangelism He will bring you closer to Himself and to the needs of man than you have ever experienced before. Write or telephone your union or conference publishing director for help in planning your best and most meaningful summer.

Section Seven

Reaching Higher, Never Satisfied

Satisfied With the Superficial

The tendency to rest satisfied with the superficial ranks highest on the scale of dangers confronting literature evangelists. It is easy to be satisfied with a shallow experience and to allow less important duties to crowd out our time with God, to neglect the very relationship that gives us Heaven's power.

In the *Review and Herald*, May 6, 1902, Ellen White emphasizes this necessity. "I speak to the workers, young and old, who are handling our books . . . : Exemplify in the life the lessons given by Christ in His sermon on the mount. This will make a deeper impression, and have a more lasting influence upon minds, than will the sermons given from the pulpit. You may not be able to speak eloquently to those you desire to help; but if you speak modestly, hiding self in Christ, your words will be dictated by the Holy Spirit; and Christ, with whom you are cooperating, will impress the heart."

Then, too, there is the danger of becoming satisfied with a superficial sales presentation. Our books today have such beautiful illustrations that we tend to sell by showing the pictures. We don't go very deep into the content. By contrast, the genius of our truly great literature evangelists has been their knowledge of their books. They could quickly turn to the precise paragraph that would meet the individual need of each prospect. They disciplined their minds to study. They memorized dozens of choice paragraphs, which at the right moment the Holy Spirit could bring to their remembrance.

More than eighty years ago Ellen White saw the danger of slipping into a pattern of the easy, superficial presentation. She warned, "In their handling of the books they [the canvassers] are being educated to present before the public the beautiful cover and many illustrations rather than the points of truth contained in the books. In doing this they are patterning after the world, and they fail to make God their dependence and trust. 'What is the chaff to the wheat?' God asks. . . . It is not the gilded leaves of a book, not the expensive covers, which testify to its value. It is the truth contained in it. This will make an impression on mind and heart."—Manuscript 131, 1899.

The evil one would like nothing better than to keep us satisfied with both our present level of spirituality and our present meager knowledge of the books we are handling. He knows that "as long as the church are satisfied with small things [or superficial things], they are disqualified to receive the great things of God" (*Review and Herald*, Nov. 15, 1892).

What can we do to squelch this sense of satisfaction with the superficial? We might try visualizing a danger signal built into the control panel of our lives. Any neglect of prayer or study would trigger a flashing light. And when we begin missing sales that should have been closed, we can picture in our mind's eye the warning signal's becoming more insistent. Deeper, still deeper, more and more knowledge is Heaven's plan for us. God's great achievers never rest satisfied with the superficial.

Set Your Mark High

Have you ever heard a literature worker resist the idea of setting goals? "Really, I don't think it's right," he rationalizes, "to tell God how much He is going to bless us. We should leave it entirely in His hands." On the other hand, we hear our most aggressive church leaders talk enthusiastically about management by objective.

Just how important is it to God for His workers to set goals and objectives? We can find answers to some of our questions in Ellen White's book *Mind, Character, and Personality,* volume 1.

Do definite goals determine success? "Success in any line demands a definite aim. He who would achieve true success in life must keep steadily in view the aim worthy of his endeavor."—Page 341. "He [Christ] would give encouragement to our loftiest aims, security to our choicest treasure."—Page 342.

How high should we aim? "Not all reach the same development or do with equal efficiency the same work. God does not expect the hyssop to attain the proportions of the cedar, or the olive the height of the stately palm. But each should aim just as high as the union of human with divine power makes it possible for him to reach."—Page 341.

What does our aimlessness do to the Holy Spirit of God? "Every soul is to minister. He is to use every physical, moral and mental power—through sanctification of the Spirit—that he may be a laborer together with God. All are bound to devote themselves actively and unreservedly to God's service. They are to cooperate with Jesus Christ in the great work of helping others. Christ died for every man. He has ransomed every man by giving His life on the cross. This He did that man might no longer live an aimless, selfish life but that he might live unto Jesus Christ, who died for his salvation. All are not called upon to enter the ministry, but nevertheless, they are to minister. It is an *insult* to the Holy Spirit of God for any man to choose a life of self-serving."—Pages 344, 345. (Italics supplied.)

Can worthy goals actually prevent evil in our lives? "One of the chief causes of mental inefficiency and moral weakness is the lack of concentration for worthy ends. . . . The mind, the heart, that is indolent, aimless, falls an easy prey to evil. It is on diseased, lifeless organisms that fungus roots. It is the idle mind that is Satan's workshop. Let the mind be directed to high and holy ideals, let the life have a noble aim, an absorbing purpose, and evil finds little foothold."—Pages 343, 344.

Inspiration makes it clear, doesn't it? God really longs for us to set high goals, to expect great achievements through His power. To do otherwise insults the Holy Spirit, who offers us unlimited assistance. God wants us to set our mark high. We must not allow any obstacle or circumstance to hold us back. "As the will of man cooperates with the will of God, it becomes omnipotent. Whatever is to be done at His command may be accomplished in His strength. All His biddings are enablings."—*Christ's Object Lessons*, p. 333.

Immeasurably More

"Now to him who is able to do immeasurably more than all we can ask or conceive . . ." (Eph. 3:20, N.E.B.).

Don't you like this glorious affirmation from God's Word? Phillips' translation expresses it even more dramatically: "[He] is able to do infinitely more than we ever dare to ask or imagine."* I like to think of this as a special promise for literature evangelists, not only for their life but also for their ministry. The Eternal Ruler of all stands ready to bless us with immeasurably more than all we can ask for or dream about.

If you let your imagination go and stretch it to its extreme limit, how much can you conceive that God could bless you in a single week? Picture it all in your mind. Dream of families responding to our message, of big sales, of cash sales, and of no cancellations. Then know that He waits to do immeasurably more.

One of the kindest and best publishing leaders I know used to always assure his colporteurs, "The Lord has many surprises for you." He was so humble that he felt he didn't really deserve the sales the Lord gave him. I had to chide him into believing that he shouldn't be surprised when sales came, that God wanted him to *expect* more, and that He wanted to give him more.

I believe that Elijah *expected* the fire to fall from heaven and consume the sacrifice. David *expected,* through the mighty power of the God of Israel, to slay Goliath. Joshua *expected* the formidable walls of Jericho to crumble and fall. Moses *expected* the path to open through the Red Sea. And today Anna-Liisa Helevaara (world-champion literature

* From J. B. Phillips: *The New Testament in Modern English,* Revised Edition, © J. B. Phillips 1958, 1960, 1972. Used by permission of Macmillan Publishing Co., Inc.

evangelist) *expects* success, even the unbelievable average of thirty-four sets of *The Bible Story* a week.

Then why aren't we achieving more? Isn't it because of our low expectations? Ellen White declared: "Many . . . accomplish little because they attempt little."—*The Ministry of Healing*, p. 498. When we expect and attempt great things, we will not be shocked or even surprised when the "immeasurably more" becomes reality.

Whenever you are tempted to think little or to attempt little, turn to these positive assurances.

"Faith looks beyond the difficulties, and lays hold of the unseen, even Omnipotence, therefore it cannot be baffled. Faith is the clasping of the hand of Christ in every emergency."—*Gospel Workers*, p. 262.

"Faith is the living power that presses through every barrier, overrides all obstacles, and plants its banner in the heart of the enemy's camp."—*Sons and Daughters of God*, p. 202.

"In the service of God there need be no despondency, no wavering, no fear. The Lord will more than fulfill the highest expectations of those who put their trust in Him."—*Prophets and Kings*, p. 387.

"When thick clouds of darkness seem to hover over the mind, then is the time to let living faith pierce the darkness and scatter the clouds. . . . I asked the angel why there was no more faith and power in Israel. He said, 'Ye let go of the arm of the Lord too soon. Press your petitions to the throne, and hold on by strong faith. The promises are sure. Believe ye receive the things ye ask for, and ye shall have them.' "—*Early Writings*, pp. 72, 73.

Every week can be a Big Week if we expect and attempt the "immeasurably more" that God longs to pour out in our lives and ministry for Him.

God and I

We would do well to frequently assess our progress—to look back and to look ahead, to look inward and then upward. We should compare that which God expected from our lives with that which He has actually received. As we contemplate both our failures and our prospects, two important attitudes will help us. They may well be two of the literature evangelist's greatest needs.

First, we must have a profound discontent with our present and past levels of achievement. As Gerald H. Bath suggests, "Perhaps psychiatrists wouldn't like the news to leak out too generally, but the truth is that the people who do most for mankind—and the happiest—are the *discontented*, people who are not satisfied with things as they are and who find happiness trying to improve them."—*Sunshine*, a Magazet, January, 1965.

Some years ago Oliver La Farge put it this way: "Were it not for the twin forces of curiosity and discontent, man would still be living in caves and brush shelters."—*Ibid*. The leaders who have brought progress to every nation on earth are those who thought things could be better and who had the spirit to do something about it. Discontent always fuels every missile of progress.

Ellen White counsels, "Be not satisfied with reaching a low standard. We are not what we might be, or what it is God's will that we should be. . . . Never think that you have learned enough, and that you may now relax your efforts."—*The Ministry of Healing*, pp. 498, 499.

In one of Adlai Esteb's best-worded poems, he asserts that little men stay little because they rest content. By contrast great men never feel satisfied. They turn their eager eyes to catch fresh visions in the skies, then stretch themselves to grasp the higher prize.

Second, we must have an absolute faith that the omnipotent God expects great things and will help us achieve great things. We must catch God's infinite vision for a finished work. We need to see what He sees for the literature ministry. We need to know what it means to Him to get *The Desire of Ages* and *The Great Controversy* into every home and to lighten every land with the glory of His permanent, printed message.

Above all, we must believe that whatever we attempt in harmony with His commands we may accomplish by His strength. "All His biddings are enablings."—*Christ's Object Lessons,* p. 333.

In an interesting allegory Lyman Abbott expresses a similar faith: "I pluck an acorn and hold it to my ear; and this is what it says to me: 'By and by the birds will come and nest in me. By and by I will furnish shade for the cattle. . . . I will provide warmth for the home. . . . By and by I will be the strong ribs of a great vessel, and the tempest will beat against me in vain, while I carry men across the great sea.'

" 'Oh, foolish little acorn, wilt thou be all this?' I ask.

"And the acorn answers, 'Yes, God and I.' "—*Sunshine,* a Magazet, January, 1962.

Jesus longs for us to possess this kind of far-seeing faith. With Him we, too, can move mountains.

Glimpses of Fire

Have you ever imagined what literature evangelism will be like under the loud-cry and latter-rain power? When the Lord gives you a little foretaste of that power, have you reacted inside: "It's so unreal. It can't be happening to me"? I felt that way in Inter-America as Elder Luis Ramirez and I touched down in the various fields of that great division.

Can you imagine a conference president meeting with his publishing director, ten associate publishing department leaders, and nearly two hundred literature evangelists, and still planning for more? It isn't a dream. It is really happening with the West Venezuela Conference president and his literature evangelist team.

Can you picture an entire union territory with one full-time literature worker for every 8,000 people? In the Caribbean Union this has already become a reality. Some of their island fields now average one colporteur for every 4,000 to 5,000 people. Yet the conference leaders are planning for more!

But above all, have you dreamed of a "leaves of autumn" sales level, of sufficient deliveries to saturate the earth with literature? This, too, is beginning to happen across Inter-America. Recently a worker in the East Puerto Rico Conference asked a customer who was a pastor if he might present the books in the pastor's church. "No," the pastor replied. "It is better if *we* go to every home." The pastor accompanied our brother to the homes of his members and urged them to buy. God's Spirit seems to be taking over. He wants to make sure that His printed message reaches every home.

These are only a few brief glimpses of the literature work in Inter-America. You have to see it to believe it. Not an isolated union or conference but an entire division is being lighted with a mighty colporteur revival.

If it can happen in Inter-America, it can happen anywhere. The Rio Grande is not wide enough to stop a program of such intensity. This is the predicted power of "that other angel" who lightens the earth with the glory of God. Like the mighty rushing wind of a Caribbean hurricane, God wants this holy zeal to sweep across North America and across every division on earth. These loud-cry dreams must burst forth into reality.

Chrematophobia

Not long ago I talked to one of our veteran literature evangelists about reaching a higher goal in deliveries. There were a number of reasons why he should improve, the first six reasons being six little children who would need a Christian education. He was doing quite well, however, and had almost completed payments on a comfortable home situated a few miles from good city territory. He replied, "You know, Elder Hunt, I think it's a little dangerous for a colporteur to earn too much money."

Perhaps he was right, but he just might have been suffering from a slight case of chrematophobia. According to a recent issue of *Sales Management* magazine, chrematophobia is the "fear of excess money." Surprising as it appears, the reports of the average literature evangelist indicate that quite a number show symptoms of this strange malady.

Such a fear should have no place in the experience of a

truly converted literature evangelist. God wants every literature evangelist to prosper and to have an abundance to give to the work of God. Isaiah 61:6 promises that "ye shall eat the riches of the Gentiles." And Malachi 3:10 states, "Prove me now herewith, saith the Lord of hosts, if I will not open you the windows of heaven, and pour you out a blessing, that there shall not be room enough to receive it."

So there is really no reason to hold back in our thinking and planning. God wants us to do great things and to reach high goals. The more money we earn, the more we can give to help finish His work. In fact, some of our most successful colporteurs give a second and even a third tithe for the support of the church and God's great mission program. The more they have to give, the wider God opens the windows of heaven.

I know from experience that His promises are sure. The first Big Week in which I dedicated a double tithe to the Lord, I realized almost double the deliveries of my previous biggest week. Try it for yourself, and allow the Lord to make you a more prosperous literature evangelist. Yes, fear lest the love of gain should taint your service, but remember that you can never get too much to give for the cause of God.

Hundreds of thousands of dollars more each year could go just toward printing the message and getting it out to the millions living on just one of the world's needy continents. So let's give a good share of our earnings to God's cause and let's receive His more abundant blessings. We need not allow chrematophobia to trouble us!

By Divine Decree

Jetzt ist die Zeit! Now is the time! This compelling cry from our General Conference world session in Vienna keeps sounding and resounding in our souls. A new spirit of revival and urgency permeates the church. Responsible men and women are planning to place the message "in every home in every land." Probation will soon close. We must give the final call, "Come out of her, my people." The time is *now!*

In *Testimonies,* volume 7, pages 138-140, Ellen White depicts the leading role that literature evangelism will play. By divine decree our publishing houses have been designed to be "among the most effective agencies" in proclaiming the hour of God's judgment and the three angels' messages. As did John the Baptist, so they are to prepare a people to meet God. "In a large degree" they will accomplish the work of that "other angel . . . who lightens the earth with his glory."

But let's get down to specifics. How can literature workers—the John the Baptists of today—fulfill their divinely predicted role? We believe that God wants an army of at least 25,000 full-time literature workers and at least 100,000 of their customers baptized during the next five years.

You can assist in reaching these goals in two ways:

1. *Watch for and encourage prospective literature workers.* Tell them how the Lord has helped you. Invite them to work with you. Let them share firsthand your happiness in heart-to-heart ministry. Ask your publishing leader to explain the work to them. He will be contacting at least four potential workers each week, until we are marching 25,000 strong. You can help your leaders find the right men and women.

2. *Make a commitment for souls.* Set aside a special day of commitment. Then on your knees plan your priorities and set

your soul-winning goals. Resolve that you will consider every customer a possible candidate for the kingdom. Ask the Lord to help you give priority to the large Spirit of Prophecy books. Determine, through these precious books and Jesus' power, to lift men and women out of Babylon, to pull them free from the old roaring lion's tenacious jaws.

Remember, at the King's command we are marching with the undefeated armies of heaven. "Angels are belting the world, refusing Satan his claims to supremacy. . . . Their hands are linked about the world, and with sleepless vigilance they are keeping the armies of Satan at bay till the sealing of God's people shall be accomplished."—*The SDA Bible Commentary*, Ellen G. White Comments, vol. 7, p. 967. Like riot police the angels are holding back Satan's angry fiends so that we may have a little more time to reach every home.

Let us go forth as conquerors. No earthly or hellish power can stop us. Our success has been decreed by Heaven. Now is the time!

A Pro's Pattern

"Winning doesn't just happen," a great pro explained. "You've got to make it happen. It isn't easy. You can't just sit and wait for it. You've got to give it everything you have." Professionals in the literature ministry would probably give the same advice. Some of our top achievers have told us how they do it. We can study their profiles carefully and develop for ourselves the pattern of the pro.

At an institute for all Scandinavia I interviewed Mrs. Anna-Liisa Helevaara, the leading worker from Finland. How can she consistently deliver more than $100,000 worth of literature each year? Here are four significant factors—the basic elements in her pattern of success.

1. *An indomitable spirit.* Mrs. Helevaara freely confesses that she has no extraordinary abilities. God called her from the Pentecostal Church and from a humble occupation. Her first job was as janitor of the Adventist church, and she used to weep for joy that she had the privilege of cleaning the floor on which God's people walked. Later in the literature ministry she sometimes worked many hours without sales. The literature work is not a pushover in Finland. Sixty percent of her sales are to atheists or Communists. God gives the victory through her positive and determined spirit.

2. *Careful management of time.* "I believe I should work for God just as many hours as I had to work for the 'Egyptians,'" explains this intrepid worker. "I canvass 20-25 homes every day." And she doesn't miss a single home. She visits mothers with children during the day and families without children during the evenings. Mrs. Helevaara breathes a short prayer outside each door. Her introduction frankly reveals that she comes from the Adventist Church.

3. *A carefully condensed sales talk.* At first Mrs. Helevaara used a regular, full-length sales talk. She kept making it shorter and shorter and now gives just the right points with crisp, clear sentences that hit the target. "No one is too old, no one is too young, for the *Bible Story.* . . . They are for children, but they are not childish." When a customer says, "I don't have the time," she quickly responds, "But you must take the time before it is too late!"

4. *Entire dependence upon God.* "For four years," Mrs. Helevaara confessed, "I went out with the spirit of fear. I was

not happy. I thought too much about myself and what the people would think of me." Then after a very hard day without a single sale, she paused, faced a high brick wall, and pleaded with God to give her the right spirit. She decided to contact two more homes. She felt God's presence with her and sold sets in both homes. That was the turning point. It was "the best day of my life, the day I started depending entirely on God," she exults. When she told her publishing director, Seppo Vehkavuori, that she was satisfied with selling one or two sets a day, he replied, "You may be satisfied, but is God satisfied?" Now her chief concern is to satisfy God. She wants Him to work through her to His glory.

Let's give God and His work everything we have. He will shape it into a real pro's pattern.

Expecting More

"Talk and act as if your faith was invincible."—*Christ's Object Lessons*, p. 147.

In the book *Evangelism*, pages 451, 452, Ellen White illustrates her positive approach in dealing with souls. An angel urged her, "'Go to Brother ———, place your books before him, and this will save his soul.'" She said that he was a man "whom, with his whole family, we highly prized." He had listened to the preaching of the truth but had slipped back into his worldly ways. Ellen White said, "I talked with him just as though he were with us." She told him that he had a responsibility to take the truth to his neighbors.

He looked at her in a strange way, as though to say, "'I do

not think you know that I have given up the truth, that I have allowed my girls to go to dances, and to the Sunday school, that we do not keep the Sabbath.'" But even though Mrs. White did know, she continued speaking with him just as though he were a member of the church. She told him she had brought him some books to use in helping his neighbors. Then she knelt down and prayed for him. "The tears were rolling down his face," she said, when they arose. He testified later that *Patriarchs and Prophets* "pulled me out of the mire." This man and his entire family took their stand for the truth, and God used them as the means of saving other families.

What might have happened had Ellen White talked as if she expected a negative response? What if she had pointed a finger at him and condemned him for what he had failed to do? Instead, she acted as if he had already made the right decision. She gave no indication of doubt. The power of positive faith, speech, and action gained the victory for God.

Workers today who are constantly in touch with Heaven will talk and act in the same positive manner. They know that Jesus will soon return and that His truth will go forward to a triumphant close. They know that He has all power. Therefore they can *never* "think, much less . . . speak, of failure in their work." Instead they respond to His earnest longing to "expect great things from Him" (*Colporteur Ministry*, pp. 118, 119).

A young minister asked the great preacher Spurgeon, "How can I have more baptisms?"

Spurgeon replied, "You don't expect to have one every week, do you?"

"No," said the young preacher.

"Then," said Spurgeon, "that's the reason you don't have more."

May this be the same reason why Adventist literature workers don't realize more baptisms from their work? And isn't this the reason why we are not selling more literature, reaching higher goals, and, most important of all, why we are not receiving more of the power of God's Spirit? God really can't give us more success or more power than we *expect* Him to give us.

The hour for the great outpouring has come. God waits with longing heart to bestow His Spirit without measure. He longs to see His literature workers *expecting* more and receiving more from His omnipotent hand. Let's talk and act positively. "All things are possible to him that believeth" (Mark 9:23).

Space Pace

In 1973, Astronauts Alan Bean, Owen Garriott, and Jack Lousma splashed down after having spent fifty-nine and a half days in space. They had traveled farther and faster than any earthborn creatures ever had. (Their record has since been surpassed.) At 17,000 miles an hour, twenty-four hours a day, they reached the staggering distance of more than 24 and a quarter million miles on a single journey! They circled the earth nearly a thousand times in less than two months. Solar physicists waited to analyze the 77,000 frames of sun pictures that the astronauts filmed through sophisticated lenses. Those photographs revealed more than all the knowledge man had discovered to that date about the sun.

In our fantastic age man seems to be blasting the top off all previous achievements or limitations. The astronauts' first footprints on lunar soil declared that the sky's no longer the limit! Nearly every category of knowledge is exploding—

breaking through all previous barriers. Everything is becoming higher, faster, bigger, or better.

Inspiration has also predicted unprecedented speed and power for the final movements of God's work. The closing message is represented by angels flying swiftly through the heavens and by streams of light going clear around the world. Even the final words of Revelation seem to urge us forward: "Surely I come quickly." The challenge to literature workers everywhere is to step up the pace. Probation soon will close. Very little time remains to reach the waiting millions. We must hurry. Even a "space pace" is almost too slow.

As we set our daily and yearly goals, let us resolve to be quick enough and high enough to meet the expectations of our King. Let us listen to His counsel: "My brethren, we have erred and sinned in attempting too little."—*Testimonies*, vol. 5, p. 391. "We want men who will push the triumphs of the cross."—*Ibid.* "His servants are constantly to enlarge the circle of their efforts. Constantly they are to do more, *never less*. The Lord's work is to widen and broaden until it encircles the world."—*Ibid.*, vol. 7, p. 15.

Unfortunately, some Christians become afflicted with acrophobia—the fear of heights. They are afraid to think big, afraid to tackle high goals. Content down on the plains of mediocre accomplishment, they allow the higher peaks to go unchallenged. God forbid that it should be true in the lives of literature workers at this hour! The heights beckon us. Inspiration urges us forward: "He [God] longs to have you expect great things from Him."—*Christ's Object Lessons*, p. 146.

The spirit of God's champions as expressed by Adlai A. Esteb must vibrate in our souls:

"Great men are never satisfied,
But look ahead and turn their eager eyes
To see fresh visions in the skies,
Then stretch themselves to grasp a higher prize."—
Scrapwood, p. 71.

Section Eight

A Universal Perspective

Indispensable Channels

One of our greatest cravings is for appreciation. We want to feel really needed, to be indispensable to a company or to a fellow human being. But isn't it infinitely more exciting to realize that the mighty God of the universe *needs us*? He is depending on us to play a crucial role in His plan.

"Is it possible," you question, "for the Omnipotent One to be dependent on His creatures for anything?" No, He is not, but in His great wisdom and love He chose to make redeemed human beings His chief instruments in reaching fallen beings. I will never forget how one Adventist writer depicted it: the angel Gabriel asks the Saviour, "Master, what if these eleven men You left on earth fail to carry out Your plans for proclaiming the gospel?" And Jesus confidently answers, "Gabriel, I have no other plan."

It is a glorious thought, isn't it? He is counting on us. He really needs us. We are indispensable to His plans for communicating His love.

Through Ellen White God emphasizes the necessity of the human channel: "God's blessings are bestowed through human instrumentality. Christ Himself came to the world as the Son of man. Humanity, united to the divine nature, must touch humanity. . . . Every individual disciple of the Master . . . is heaven's appointed channel for the revelation of God to men."—*Thoughts From the Mount of Blessing*, p. 40.

"He might dispense with ministers altogether and make

angels the ambassadors of His truth. He might have written the truth upon the firmament, or imprinted it upon the leaves of the trees and upon the flowers of the field; or He might with an audible voice have proclaimed it from heaven. But the all-wise God did not choose any of these ways. He knew that man must have something to do in order that life might be a blessing to him."—*Testimonies*, vol. 4, p. 473.

"As His representatives among men, Christ does not choose angels who have never fallen, but human beings, men of like passions with those they seek to save. Christ took upon Himself humanity, that He might reach humanity. Divinity needed humanity; for it required both the divine and the human to bring salvation to the world. Divinity needed humanity, that humanity might afford a channel of communication between God and man. . . . With almost impatient eagerness the angels wait for our cooperation; for man must be the channel to communicate with man."—*The Desire of Ages*, pp. 296, 297.

How wonderful! The Lord of glory commands the angels to speak through us. He has made us His indispensable channels to communicate His truth to others. We must not keep the angels waiting.

Jesus' Deepest Longing

Millenniums of sin had deepened the hurt and longing of the Saviour's heart. By every means in His divine soul He had sought to direct fallen mankind to the only Source of help.

Through symbols and prophets He repeatedly attempted to attract sinners to their Sin-bearer. Finally, to make sure that He would break through to man's heart He stepped down from the throne of heaven and humbled Himself to be born into the human family.

But when "he came unto his own, . . . his own received him not" (John 1:11). The angels who with hearts aflame declared the glad tidings of Jesus' birth were astonished that only a humble few in Israel were looking for His coming. "Jerusalem was not preparing to welcome her Redeemer. . . . Hearts selfish and world-engrossed were untouched by the joy that thrilled all heaven."—*The Desire of Ages*, p. 44. Even in Bethlehem, "the city of their royal line, Joseph and Mary are unrecognized and unhonored" *(ibid.)*.

Neither did Jesus' own brothers and townspeople accept Him. "They [Jesus' brothers] were jealous of Him, and manifested the most decided unbelief and contempt."—*Ibid.*, p. 87. They sneered at His unselfishness and integrity. They called His kindness cowardice. No doubt His tender heart often ached for those nearest Him who were too proud to let Him be their Saviour. Later the people of Nazareth wondered at His gracious words, but they resisted the idea of being prisoners in need of deliverance from evil. "Their pride was offended. . . . The words of Jesus indicated that His work for them was to be altogether different from what they desired."—*Ibid.*, p. 237.

And during Jesus' final hours of agony, amid jeers, mockery, and curses, He was still hoping to hear a kind word of reassurance. "With longing heart He . . . listened for some expression of faith from His disciples. He . . . heard only the mournful words, 'We trusted that it had been he which should have redeemed Israel.' How grateful then to the Saviour was the utterance of faith and love from the dying thief!"—*Ibid.*, p. 750. As Jesus' parched lips spoke the reassuring reply, His sorrowful, blood-stained face brightened with the light of heaven. A thief had granted that which He craved most—appreciative response to His saving mission and recognition of man's utter helplessness without His power.

Don't you think heaven still stands amazed that we finite human beings, in our proud independence, permit Jesus to do so little when He longs to do so much? Think back over this past year. Didn't most of your victories come when you recognized your weakness and relied entirely on His saving power?

David made it clear that God doesn't want that which glorifies the works of man. "No, I don't need your sacrifices of flesh and blood. What I want from you is your true thanks. . . . *I want you to trust me in your times of trouble, so I can rescue you, and you can give me glory*" (Ps. 50:13-15, T.L.B.).

Yes, Jesus hungers for true appreciation. He craves our surrender and dependence. He longs to reveal His glorious power in our lives. Let's make sure that we are satisfying Jesus' greatest longing!

Straightening Pictures and Priorities

Sometimes it takes a pointed illustration to lift us out of our little nests of self-satisfaction. Noted Christian writer Corrie Ten Boom uses one that haunted me. Perhaps it will haunt your soul too. She talks about Christians who are like firemen straightening the pictures on the walls of a burning house. Disregarding the shrieks of the dying inhabitants, the firemen turn aside to the ridiculously unimportant.

It's a pathetic sight. Grown men on an urgent rescue mission being diverted by trivia! Could anything be more repugnant to anyone possessing a sense of decency or duty? "Be careful now," you say. "Isn't this a bit harsh for workers who are already devoting their lives to God's service?" Perhaps, but I believe that even dedicated literature evangelists must struggle with the inclinations to straightening during a time of crisis. We often fiddle around with the *easy* while we neglect the really *important.* It takes discipline to keep on rescuing families from Satan's hellish fires. It involves some sweat and tears, a blackened face, or a singed eyebrow. So many tasks are so much easier and less trying! God's literature evangelist firemen must choose the important, choose to take the risk, choose to break through these walls of fire every hour of every day at every home.

But the lure of the *easy* always lurks nearby. Dozens of easier, and seemingly urgent, duties beckon to us. So many pictures need straightening! *That "Do" list, those things I promised I wouldn't put off another week. And it's so much easier to advertise. Leads won't come in unless I get the advertising out. I'll make the sales calls tomorrow. Right now I have to pick up the children at the church school.*

Satan chuckles as he sees his ploy working. "Time is short; the enemy will make every effort to magnify in our minds matters of lesser consequence, and to lead us to regard lightly the very work that most needs to be done."—*Colporteur Ministry,* p. 38. He will do anything to keep us from breaking through those walls of fire so we can rescue perishing souls.

Every literature evangelist needs to face up to this problem. To what am I devoting my time and life? Am I spending too much time with the *easy* and not enough time with the *important?* Do I give priority to that which Heaven counts most important?

"The true ambassador of Christ is in perfect union with Him whom He represents, and his engrossing object is the salvation of souls. The wealth of earth dwindles into insignificance when compared with the worth of a single soul for whom our Lord and Master died."—*Testimonies*, vol. 4, p. 261.

"When the atonement is viewed correctly, the salvation of souls will be felt to be of infinite value. In comparison with the enterprise of everlasting life, every other sinks into insignificance."—*The Sufferings of Christ*, p. 46.

"To every soul that accepts Jesus the cross of Calvary speaks: 'Behold the worth of the soul. "Go ye into all the world, and preach the gospel to every creature."' Nothing is to be permitted to hinder this work. It is the all-important work for time; it is to be far-reaching as eternity."—*Testimonies*, vol. 5, p. 456.

There we have it. The divine Fire Chief speaks. We must not fuss around with the easy and the inconsequential. We must seize our axes and water hoses—our briefcases loaded with books that contain the sword of truth and the water of life—and run to rescue perishing souls. We must make sure that every hour of every day is wholly devoted to the one all-absorbing priority of life. In comparison with this every other enterprise sinks into insignificance.

God's Moment

Never had the world witnessed such a glorious scene of triumph. Mighty shouts of "Hosanna!" echoed from hill to hill. The King of heaven was returning to Jerusalem. A multitude of captives whom He had freed from Satan's power surrounded Him. The blind whom He had restored to sight led the way. The dumb whose tongues He had loosed shouted the loudest hosannas. The crippled whom He had healed bounded with joy. The lepers whom He had cleansed spread their untainted garments in His path. And when the Pharisees attempted to still them, Jesus replied, "'I tell you, if my disciples keep silence the stones will shout aloud'" (Luke 19:40, N.E.B.).

But the scene of rejoicing quickly changed. The entire procession paused. From the brow of the hill they looked down on the glorious white stone walls and the sparkling gold-capped pillars of the Temple. All watched with amazement as the eyes of Israel's King filled with tears and a wail of anguish burst from His quivering lips: "'If only you had known, on this great day, the way that leads to peace!'" Then Jesus pictured the siege that would "'not leave you one stone standing on another, because you did not recognize God's moment when it came'" (Luke 19:42, 44, N.E.B.).

Today we face another glorious moment in God's great prophetic timetable. God's Son will soon make His triumphal reentry to earth. Another mighty tidal wave of hosannas must sweep across every land, reaching every home. The voices proclaiming Heaven's final "loud cry" of the third angel cannot be silenced. No army of men or demons can stop it. If they attempt to thwart it or if we remain silent, God will shout aloud through inanimate stones.

Do you feel the compelling power of this mighty publishing movement? Do you recognize that God's moment has come? Have you caught the spirit of the closing work described by Ellen White: "The heavenly messengers seen by Ezekiel, like a bright light going among the living creatures *with the swiftness of lightning*, represent the speed with which this work will finally go forward to completion."—*The SDA Bible Commentary*, Ellen G. White Comments, vol. 4, p.

1161. (Italics supplied.)

Are you keeping pace with the angels? Does our report sometimes indicate a lack of urgency? Are you reaching the number of people God wants you to reach every day? Or are you leisurely following up a few leads just as though you had a temporal millennium to complete the task? Don't you think our Saviour feels hurt today and with tears of disappointment laments, "You're not recognizing God's moment"?

God's moment *has* come! Let us show that we believe it by our daily and weekly reports. With earnest zeal let us hurry to the homes still unwarned. Jesus will lead us forward, and our faces will reflect the light of His approving smile. Let us never make it necessary for Him to put voices in stones!

Steve's Solo

"Say, Steve, do you think you could *drive* the car around the house to the hose and give it a good wash?" I was trying to inveigle our 13-year-old son into doing one of those not-so-welcome weekly chores. As he had not yet soloed, I knew it was a bit risky, but I wanted to get in some much-needed reading time.

"OK, Dad, where are the keys?" he responded according to plan. Then visibly hiding his surprise at my sudden confidence, but beaming like a 4-year-old on his first merry-go-round ride, Steve slid behind the controls of our new Ford. After several rather jerky starts and stops—"to get it in just the right position"—Steve soon absorbed himself in the less hazardous sponge-and-spray part of the task.

I congratulated myself on my salesmanship as I disappeared into the living room to the quiet seclusion of my favorite chair. "Just to get to drive the car around the block," I chuckled to myself, "that boy would wash it every day!"

Twenty minutes later I was aroused by the *br-r-r-r* and roar from too much starter and overacceleration. "Joe, are you sure he can do it by himself?" my wife anxiously called from the kitchen.

"Don't worry, honey. He'll manage it." I tried to sound reassuring. But as the car lurched into reverse and swerved in the wrong direction she screamed, "Look out! The clothesline po——!"

"*Cr-r-rrunch!*" I could hear the scraping and crumpling of the bright, new right rear fender as it made contact with the metal clothesline post.

As my feet thumped to the carpet they were already desperately flailing in the direction of the back door. Arriving too late to help, I joined a distressed mother and a very subdued teen-age son.

Then postmortem-like, after considerable muttering and lamenting over my foolhardy mistake, I blurted out, "I shouldn't have given him the keys. Not until he's at least ——"

"Don't be too hard on him," my wife soothingly interrupted. "He's got to learn sometime."

"That's true, but this Ford's got too much power." I glanced at Steve to make sure he was listening. "He's not ready for it yet."

Could this be the reason our heavenly Father hesitates to impart more of His blessings and power to some of His earthly children? Has He already seen in our lives too many "crumpled fenders"—the results of the selfish misappropriation of His gifts? Yet all the power He can safely trust us to use for His glory and for the benefit of mankind He will abundantly bestow. How much longer must He wait before He can trust us with the keys?

Safari Surprise

With our cameras cocked and our telephoto lenses in position, we started out on another fascinating lap of our Uganda safari. Elders D. R. L. Astleford, George Huse, and I were squeezing into our schedule a one-day interlude at the famous Murchison Game Lodge. Chugging across the Nile channel on a two-car ferry, we watched intently for hippo "islands" or crocodile "logs" on the river's smooth surface.

When our Austin bumped off the ferry and gained momentum amid clouds of copper-red dust, I wondered aloud, "What'll it be today? Every time we come we see something we've never seen before."

"Surely hope we run into another big herd of elephants!" D.R.L. grinned. "The ranger says there are seven thousand in this reserve."

But our surprise didn't come until we skidded to a halt at the tsetse-fly-control barrier. As the khaki-uniformed officers started their spray-and-inspection ritual a villager of noble bearing, clad in colorful chief's regalia, suddenly appeared before us.

"What in the world——?" Elder Huse's question was interrupted by our visitor's cheerful Swahili words, "*Jambo, Bwana!*" (Hello, Sir!) "*Habari gani leo?*" (What's the news today?) Our eyes danced with the delightful reflections of an imposing headdress lined with rainbow-colored plumes and a garb of shiny black-and-gold leopard skin. From the top feather to the beaded sandals he met every specification of a real-life African chief.

Almost immediately, however, he held up a well-worn box with a slot in the top. Across its front in poorly painted letters a few misspelled English words confessed his true status in life. We chuckled as we read, "I am not a cheef. I am a baggar." Like the bursting of an overinflated balloon, our image of his chieftainship shattered and disappeared. He was just a clever, prosperous panhandler!

Motoring on toward Kampala, I thought of the safari of life and its many surprises. The world seems bent on lauding the externals, the bright "plumes" and the prosperous "skins" of outward achievement. But God sees through the guise and "looketh on the heart." He sees the emptiness of soul and the inward spiritual poverty. And if only I ask, the great Chief of heaven will refashion this beggarly heart of mine into a heart like His, one that shall forever reflect His princely glory.

Other Worlds Watching

Have you ever noticed how well a team performs at its home stadium, how often it goes beyond its usual ability? So many thousands of loyal fans are cheering the players on to victory that they simply *have* to win!

Shouldn't we thrill with the same enthusiastic resolve about the great game our God has asked us to play? This world is really His stadium, the home stadium for heaven and the unfallen worlds. Sister White calls it "the lesson book of the universe" (*Patriarchs and Prophets*, p. 154). And the contest is very real. Satan, with his opposing team, plays "with extensive, well-organized plans and marvelous power" (*ibid.*, p. 78). His team, defiant and determined, constantly resorts to cheating and treachery in order to win.

On the other hand, God's team, the carefully selected "home team" of heaven, will play only fair and clean. "In dealing with evil His plans were far-reaching and comprehensive."—*Ibid.* He must "demonstrate to all the universe the nature of the rebellion" (*ibid.*). The stakes are high, and God must make sure that victory is complete and for eternity.

And the unfallen spectators of the universe root for His side. "The holy inhabitants of other worlds were watching with the deepest interest the events taking place on the earth."—*Ibid.* "God carries with Him the sympathy and approval of the whole universe as step by step His great plan advances to its complete fulfillment. He will carry it with Him in the final eradication of rebellion."—*Ibid.*, p. 79.

It's a glorious thought, isn't it? We are members of God's team, the home team of heaven! And from the celestial grandstands of the universe billions of sinless intelligences are watching. They are cheering us forward in our great contest with the forces of evil. They are watching and applauding, just as they did when Abraham climbed Mount Moriah. "All heaven beheld with wonder and admiration Abraham's unfaltering obedience. All heaven applauded his fidelity."—*Ibid.*, p. 155. "The whole universe is watching with inexpressible interest the closing scenes of the great controversy between good and evil."—*Prophets and Kings*, p. 148.

As members of heaven's home team, we ought to play as for our very lives. Our Captain's own character, His law, His love, have been called into question. His honor must be vindicated. His plan for redeeming man must be proved adequate, complete, and eternally successful. Let's move forward, then, as "those who will work as if they could see the heavenly universe watching them" (*Colporteur Ministry*, p. 112). Let's go out to battle like Jehoshaphat's army when it faced a "great horde" of the enemy. Despite the foe, Jahaziel praised God for victory, declaring, "The battle is not your's, but God's" (2 Chron. 20:15).

Billions of unfallen beings are on our side! We cannot fail! Let's shout it with Elisha—"Fear not: for they that be with us are more than they that be with them" (2 Kings 6:16).